COASTAL VILLAGES

Liv Kennedy

Harbour Publishing

Second printing (revised) 1992

Published by
HARBOUR PUBLISHING
P.O. Box 219
Madeira Park, BC Canada V0N 2H0

Edited by Daniel Francis
Design by Fiona MacGregor
Maps drawn by Nola Johnston

Photograph source credits: BCARS — British Columbia Archives & Records Service; CRM — Campbell River Museum; PAC — Public Archives of Canada; VPL — Vancouver Public Library. All contemporary photographs not otherwise credited are by Liv Kennedy.

Canadian Cataloguing in Publication Data

Kennedy, Liv
Coastal villages

Includes bibliographical references and index.
ISBN 1-55017-057-0

1. Pacific Coast (B.C.) — History. 2. Villages — British Columbia — Pacific Coast — History. 3. British Columbia — History, Local.
I. Title.
FC3817.4.K45 1991 971.1'1 C91-091673-X
F1087.K45 1991

This book was written with the assistance of a Canada Council Non-Fiction Book Award, and financial assistance was also received from the Department of the Secretary of State, Canada, Office of Multi-Culturalism.

Printed in Canada

To my mother and father
who pioneered this coast

To my husband Hugh and son Curtis
whose continuous support
has made it possible
for me to finish this book

Contents

Preface

I was born on the coast of British Columbia and brought up in its logging camps and fishing villages.

My father, Ingebrigt Hansen, left his home in the Lofoten Islands, Norway, in 1883, at the age of fourteen, to sail before the mast. He spent twenty years working under sail, from cabin boy to captain. In his quest to see the world he rounded Cape Horn, the southernmost tip of South America, many times.

Vancouver was a frequent port of destination. My father was impressed by the beauty of the surrounding coast with its forests and mountains. It reminded him of his homeland. Near the turn of the century he took a break from the sea and went logging where North Vancouver is today. But the ocean beckoned, and like many true sailors, he returned to the ships for another fifteen years.

During World War I he served in the US Coast Guard, and then returned to the Lofotens where he met and married my mother, Ferdinanda Maria-Louise Mattisen. Back in British Columbia, he took a job in a logging camp at Port Neville. Six years later,

in the summer of 1925, my mother and my eldest sister Edith, who was born in Norway, joined my father. They had sailed to Montreal, crossed Canada by train, and taken the Union Steamship to Port Neville.

It was along the coast of British Columbia between 1926 and 1946 that my sisters and brother, Louise, Inamar and Ingolf, and I were born. Ina and Ingolf were born at St. Michaels, the hospital at Rock Bay, and Louise and I were born aboard the Coast Mission ship *Columbia*, which had a doctor and operating room aboard.

During those years we lived at Port Neville, Hardwicke Island, Sayward, Loughborough Inlet, Owen Bay, and our homestead on northern Quadra Island between Chonat and Pulton bays. The last place we lived before moving to Vancouver was Redonda Bay.

I returned to these places for the first time in 1964. Since then I have cruised the coast extensively, taking photographs and talking to people, and writing this book. My intent has been to record in words and pictures the history of some of the early settlements along the

Far left: The photograph of my father Ingebrigt Hansen (at left) and a shipmate was taken while he was serving with the US Coast Guard during World War One. When the war ended, he went back to Norway, married my mother and re-settled in Canada.

Left: My mother Ferdinanda Hansen stands in her garden at our homestead on northern Quadra Island. Sonora Island and the Okisollo Channel are in the background. It was customary for my mother to give flowers, fruit and vegetables to visitors.

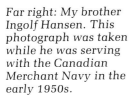

Right: My elder sister Louise and myself in the buggy, bundled up beneath a Norwegian Hardanger cloth made by my mother.

Far right: My brother Ingolf Hansen. This photograph was taken while he was serving with the Canadian Merchant Navy in the early 1950s.

coast, providing insights into life in small coastal communities in the late nineteenth and early twentieth centuries.

This imaginary cruise along the "once upon a time" coast begins at Lund and the Wishbone on the Malaspina Peninsula, and from there travels to Campbell River on Vancouver Island, southern Quadra, and the villages of Desolation Sound. We then journey north through Hoskyn Channel and Surge Narrows to Owen Bay, and then through the Hole-in-the-Wall and Yucultas to Stuart Island. From there the cruise continues northward through Calm and Chancellor Channels to the Johnstone Straits, exploring the villages, fishing camps and tiny outposts along the way as far north as Cascade Harbour and Shushartie Bay.

The photographs are an essential part of the record; they reflect the starkly impressive scenery that shaped the consciousness of the inhabitants of these communities. I have also used many of the old diaries, photographs and maps that are still in the hands of descendants of the original settlers. Most important, I have visited these communities and recorded the recollections of surviving pioneers before they are lost forever.

I would like to thank two of my friends for their special help in writing this book: Ybo Lalau, for generously sharing his yacht *Jubilee*, which made it possible for me to visit many of the more remote village sites; and Gerry Kidd, the founding publisher of *Pacific Yachting* and the present publisher of *Boat World*, who has supported and encouraged my writing for many years.

Left: My son Curtis, myself and my former husband Charles Kennedy aboard our thirty-seven-foot sailboat Kelea, dockside in Durban Harbour, 1967. We spent fourteen months in South Africa. Charles, an engineering pattern maker, found work there while I continued working as a writer. Curtis, then in grade seven, attended public school, taking Afrikaans as a second language.

1. The Coast of British Columbia

Coastal British Columbia has its own distinctive environment, shaped by the irresistible force of the great Pacific Ocean meeting the Canadian Cordillera. During the ice ages, long before mankind saw these shores, the glaciers carved steep-sided valleys into the mountains. When the glaciers receded, they left behind deep inlets, small bays and thousands of islands.

Through the ages, the mountains wrung generous amounts of rain from the Pacific winds, nurturing the growth of a dense, temperate rain forest. The sea, encircling its many inlets and rocky islands, teemed with marine life. For the early native inhabitants, these resources were reliable providers of food and shelter.

In the temperate coastal climate, looking after life's basic necessities was easy enough that the early inhabitants developed the richest and most varied native cultures in Canada. Because of the abundant natural resources and the natives' spiritual traditions, there were huge stands of mighty Douglas fir and shining shoals of salmon leaping up the rivers to spawn — even after thousands of years of human occupation.

In the early part of this century, millions of acres of Crown land were available to settlers. All that was necessary to establish a pre-emption, providing the land was unoccupied, was to blaze a "witness tree" on the corner of the lot and make a rough description of the 160 acres to be homesteaded. The land cost one dollar, providing the homesteader cleared ten acres in ten years and lived on the land for at least six months out of every year. When the homesteader had blazed his tree, he rowed back to Vancouver or Victoria and presented his claim to the government for validation, then headed back up the coast with his wife and children and all their belongings. Few of these people have been written about. They are the subject of this book.

From the middle of the nineteenth century to the late 1940s, the coast of British Columbia was settled by newcomers from all parts of the world. Some of them homesteaded, while others settled in established villages. Their livelihood came from fishing, logging, mining and trapping. Homes were built of logs or from planks and shakes cut by hand or purchased from small coastal mills. Wood stoves, oil lamps and nearby streams provided all the

amenities these pioneers needed.

Not all of the pioneers were bachelors, but generally the men went ahead to scout out the land before having their women join them. Some of them spent several months and rowed hundreds of miles in search of a good place to settle. It was a hard life, especially for the women, who often came from large cities to join their adventure-seeking husbands. Many were forced to raise their children far from the nearest doctor, dentist or school.

There were plenty of loners among the first non-native settlers on the coast. They had come from the United States, Europe and Asia, and they were farmers, labourers, tradesmen and sailors. Some were veterans of the United States Civil War. Some were intellectuals; others were drifters who had come to BC in search of freedom and a better way of life. They prospected or hand-logged in some little bay where they built a shack on the beach and lived off the land in peace.

Transportation was essential to survival. Before the turn of the century and for many years afterwards, the pioneers of the coast relied on the rowboat. Some settlers' only contact with the rest of the world was their rowboat, which could usually be seen pulled up on the beach near their homestead. I have a photograph, taken in 1919, of my father standing beside his clinker-built rowboat. It was with great pride that he sent the picture to his brother Anton in Seattle. On the back he wrote in Norwegian, "I now have a little boat."

What boats they had generally depended on

When my father Ingebrigt came to Canada in 1919, he had little money. It was with great pride that he sent a copy of this picture to his brother Anton in Seattle, Washington, letting him know that he had purchased a sixteen-foot rowboat. My father (at right) is standing in the boat with the cook for the logging camp where he was working.

what they could afford. Some had dugout canoes built by native Indians. Those with more cash had clinker-built boats about sixteen feet long, similar to a ship's lifeboat. The dugout canoes were good little sea boats but they had little room for storage. The larger clinker-built boats were not only good sea boats but there was room to stretch a tarp across the gunwales to make a dry place to sleep at night. They sometimes provided a home for many months, even years.

Most of these boats had masts and sails that could be raised when winds were favourable. They were generally cutter-rigged and carried makeshift sails of sugar sacks and old clothing sewn together. Some of the early navigators were lucky enough to get a piece of canvas from one of the sailing ships in the Port of Vancouver. They carried a bedroll, an axe, hammer and nails, a good knife, fishing gear, sometimes a gun, warm clothing, needle and thread, pencil and paper, matches and flint, a fork and spoon, a couple of pots for cooking and maybe a frying pan, a coal-oil lantern, fuel, rope and personal belongings such as family photographs and important papers.

Not many immigrants who came to settle in British Columbia were oarsmen. They were incapable of journeying hundreds of miles in a small, open boat; that was something they had to learn later. They had little idea of the vastness of the country into which they were moving, and even less knowledge of how to reach the land that had been assigned to them. To make life even more difficult, their first language was often not English. To overcome these handicaps, they sometimes pooled whatever money they had and hired an agent to

help them. The agent negotiated the charter of a steam tug or small supply vessel to take them to their new homesites along the coast.

In 1887, to help meet the demand for passenger service, the Hudson's Bay Company brought the fifty-year-old paddle-wheeler *Beaver* back into service. Unfortunately, within a year the *Beaver* foundered on the rocks off Prospect Point in what is now Stanley Park. A year later, in 1889, the Union Steamship Company was incorporated by a group of Vancouver businessmen. It began operating a number of passenger and supply vessels to serve the isolated areas of the coast, starting with a fleet of three tugs and eight barges. For the next seventy years, the Union steamships were the main contact villagers had with the outside world. The captains, mates and crews of these ships were as much a part of coastal life as the people who lived there. No matter how small the community, sometimes even a single dwelling, it would not be forgotten by the kindly skippers.

Even with the Union steamships, other supply vessels and the Columbia Coast Mission boats operating on the coast, the rowboat remained one of the most important possessions a settler had. It was a long time before the first gas boats arrived, and even then the rowboat was often more reliable. Fred Kohse, one of the best-known fishermen along this coast, recalls when he was a young man living near Kelsey Bay, rowing and sailing the long stretch of rough water to fish off the mouth of Knight Inlet eighty-five miles away.

When we were children living at our homestead on northern Quadra Island, during the early 1940s, my sisters and I took our rowboats and picked up logs that had broken away from their booms during a storm. Sometimes it took several hours to tow the logs ashore, where we tied them in front of our dock. A few days later, a tug would come down the channel looking for the breakaways, spot some of them at our dock and come to collect them. They paid us a dollar a log. Not much when you consider that some of the logs were six feet in diameter and worth a lot of money even then. However, for us it was one way to make some spending money. Several years later, I visited a physician for a hand injury, and he looked at my hands and said, "You must have done a lot of rowing when you were a youngster."

Logging was a major industry along the BC coast in the early days, partly because it was so easy to start a small logging operation. The procedure was similar to the pre-emption system for settlers: a would-be logger installed a corner post or blazed a "witness tree" on any unoccupied Crown land. He then composed a rough description of the square mile of the forest cornered on that point, and secured exclusive timber rights. Large syndicates or companies acquired almost unlimited timber

Horse logging or logging with oxen was the principal means of taking logs out of the forest. Logs were winched onto a sled, then hauled over greased skids to the water. (VPL 97)

An early version of a boom boat (centre foreground) pushes logs into place to form a boom. These small boats were made famous at Expo 86 in Vancouver when they performed "The Boom-Boat Ballet." (Dave Roels photo, courtesy Council of Forest Industries)

licences by paying an annual royalty on the value of the timber actually cut. As well, they bought timber rights from settlers.

Many smaller camps, and even some larger ones, were built on floats so they could be moved easily to a new area when a place was logged out. Most of the houses on the coast at that time were built on skids, and if they were not already on a float they could be hauled onto one if the owner wanted to relocate. Even today, especially with the growth of fish farming, you will find many floating villages along the coast.

During the first half of this century it was hand-logging and "gyppo" logging that attracted a lot of settlers to the coast. The hand-logger set up his operation where a good stand of timber grew close to a sheltered bay that

Tugboats are still used to tow log booms from logging sites to sawmills along the BC coast.

The Jennie F Decker, *a Gloucester schooner of the type used at the beginning of the commercial halibut industry.*

could be used as a booming ground. He either felled the trees directly into the water or, if most of the trees were inland, he built a log chute, winched the limbed trees to the chute and skidded them into the water. The term "gyppo" was not a reflection on the logger's business ethics. It was simply a way of describing a small-scale operation with only a few people and no heavy equipment.

At the other end of the scale were companies like Merrill, Ring and Wilson, one of the largest logging operations on the coast during the first half of this century. It used locomotives to haul out timber to its headquarters at Rock Bay, about twenty-five miles north of Campbell River. As the centre of the operation, Rock Bay became a bustling village with stores, hotels, a school and a post office to serve the men and their families working in the camp and the woods.

Accidents are fairly frequent and generally serious in the logging industry, and a hospital was something that Rock Bay lacked. The nearest one was at Campbell River, but dangerous tidal currents in Seymour Narrows made water travel to Campbell River hazardous. The hospital at Alert Bay was about seventy miles north along the storm-swept Johnstone Strait. The Mission boat *Columbia* was equipped only for minor surgery. The geography of the coast made Rock Bay far easier to reach for people who lived north of Sey-

mour Narrows and got around by small boat.

The Columbia Coast Mission, which operated the hospital at Alert Bay, saw the urgent need for another one at Rock Bay. They built St. Michael's Hospital there in 1911, and staffed it with well-trained doctors and nurses who at times seemed to perform miracles. I can recall a number of emergency trips my family made to that hospital.

One time while we were living on the homestead on Quadra Island, my mother began hemorrhaging and had to get to a doctor quickly. Only my mother and I were home at the time. Who knows what the outcome would have been had a friend not pulled into our dock in a small motorboat and offered to take my mother to the hospital. The boat was capable of doing about fifteen knots, but as we were heading into a strong northwesterly the ten-mile stretch took most of the day. The boat had no windshield. Every wave poured in over the bow. I bailed and tried to comfort my mother while the owner of the boat kept it on course. Luckily the engine kept running!

Today there is little that remains of that once-thriving community at Rock Bay. The woods operation ceased in the early 1940s. The hospital remained open a few more years but eventually had financial difficulties and closed its doors. Slowly the people moved away. Rock Bay became a ghost town. The buildings were destroyed by fire in the late

Above: Dory fishermen hauling in the groundline with a hand gurdy, 1914. (BCARS 83697)

Below: Gillnetting with sailboats at the "Glory Hole," Kennedy Island, Skeena River, 1920. (BCARS 31216)

Zellerbach and BC Forest Products took over most of the forest licences. Today most logging on the coast is done on a big scale.

The fishing industry has gone through similar changes. The aboriginal inhabitants of the coast took the bulk of their food from the sea. Fishing and gathering other seafood occupied a primary place in their culture and technology. Salmon, fresh and dried, was the staple of their diet. The little eulachon, or candlefish, provided the oil with which the Indians dressed their fish and other food. When the first Europeans arrived, the Indians shared with them their knowledge of the fishing grounds. They taught the newcomers their fishing techniques and showed them how to erect weirs across rivers during the salmon-spawning run.

The Hudson's Bay Company began trading with the natives to procure dried fish for food at its posts, supplying them in return with steel hooks and twine for nets that increased the effectiveness of their fishery. As early as the 1830s, the HBC established a saltery on the San Juan Islands to barrel salted salmon for trade with the Hawaiian Islands and Asia. The trade was small, and Europe was too far away to make the shipment of cured salmon economical. The saltery closed when the United States took possession of the San Juans in 1858.

By that time a California company was developing a method to can west coast salmon, and by 1862 a cannery opened on the Columbia River. The first salmon cannery in British

1940s. The railway trestles rotted into the ground. Even the big wharf where the Union steamships docked and other ships loaded lumber, was reclaimed by the sea.

As technology progressed, the horse and ox were replaced by the steam donkey, and in bigger operations locomotives hauled out the logs. These methods in turn were supplanted by truck logging and logging by helicopter. The day of the gyppo and hand-logger was phased out in the early 1950s. Giant forest companies like MacMillan-Bloedel, Crown

Longlining a grey cod and a halibut, 1914. Note the gurdy on the left for hauling in the line and the gurdy side roll on the rail at the right. (BCARS 83713)

Columbia was started on the Fraser River in 1870 by Alexander Loggie & Company. Methods were primitive and there was little market for the product until the transcontinental railway was completed in 1886 and the newly formed city of Vancouver expanded its docking facilities.

The clipper ship *Titania* cleared the port of Vancouver for England with a full cargo of canned salmon in 1889. Four years later a trainload of canned salmon was shipped to eastern Canada by the Anglo-British Columbia Packing Company, and from there to Britain via Atlantic ports. This was the beginning of the west coast commercial salmon fishery.

At first, European settlers were not attracted to cannery work. Logging, work on the railway or searching for gold were more lucrative. Statistics of those employed by the industry in 1884 were as follows: 1,280 Indians, 1,153 Chinese, 273 "whites." After the gold fever ran its course, however, the picture changed and Europeans discovered there were good jobs — even fortunes to be made — in the fishing industry. Norwegians, Scots, Greeks, Yugoslavs, Finns, Newfoundlanders, Nova Scotians, Japanese, Greeks, French and Irish joined west coast Indians in bringing in the precious harvest from the sea. American prospectors who came to find gold stayed on to prospect the sea instead.

As mechanization increased, large corporations came to dominate the industry. In 1891, the Anglo-BC Packing Company built nine canneries. In 1902, the BC Packers Association was founded. By 1940, BC Packers had built some forty-one canneries along the coast.

Canneries built on remote stretches of the coast had their building supplies shipped in by tug and barge. Besides the plant, each cannery was a whole village, including a company store, cookhouse and housing for workers and management. As well there was a separate village for Chinese employees.

There was cannery work for both men and women. The men worked mostly on the boats or on repairs and maintenance. The women washed and cleaned the salmon, then packed the fish pieces into cans after the Chinese workers had done the butchering. When the

A "whale" of a halibut on the Andrew Kelly, *1914. (BCARS 83711)*

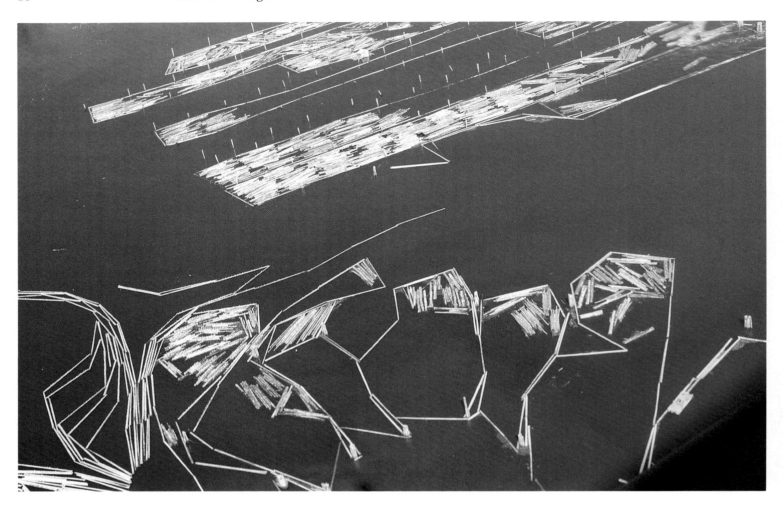

Pattern of log booms on the BC coast.

industry became more mechanized, women operated the canning machines.

My sisters and I worked in some of the canneries during the late 1940s. We were teenagers and still in school, but it was a better way to make spending money than towing in logs.

We were living in Redonda Bay when we decided to write to the Canadian Fishing Company and ask for employment in one of its canneries. You can imagine our excitement when a couple of weeks later we received a reply offering us work at Goose Bay Cannery

A self-loading log barge heading south in Discovery Passage.

Homfray Channel and the head of Pendrell Sound in the heart of Desolation Sound. (George McNutt photo)

in Rivers Inlet. The pay was forty-five cents an hour, but the bonus was that the company paid our fare from Redonda Bay to Rivers Inlet and covered expenses in Vancouver while we waited for a steamship to take us north. The trip from Vancouver to Goose Bay took four days, with stops at many small outposts along the coast. We had friends in some of these places and could go ashore for a visit while freight and passengers were unloaded.

At Goose Bay we got to know some of the people at the Chinese village, and on special occasions we were invited to participate in some of their elaborate banquets. That was my introduction to the Chinese way of cooking. We also spent one summer working at the Bones Bay cannery on East Cracroft Island. One of the highlights of that summer was

Right: Rainbow Theatre was a puppet show given in a shingle cabin built over the decks of a catamaran hull. The vessel, named Jonathan Livingston Seagull II, was built in Finn Bay. The owner, Sean Livingston Kent, was a professional actor who travelled the coast with his shows during the 1980s.

Salmon gillnet skiffs on an outgoing tow, Kibella Bay, Rivers Inlet, 1930. (Philip J. Thomas photo)

Right: Salmon gillnetting on the Fraser River. (BCARS 72291)

Below: Linen nets were mended for about four or five hours on Saturday mornings. They were soaked for an hour in a bluestone solution before being returned to the gillnetters. (PAC 40981)

going to the dances at Sointula. I have many happy memories of the days I worked in the canneries. Indeed, I feel very fortunate to have grown up in that part of the century.

Early this century it was the gillnet fishermen in rowboats who supplied the canneries with salmon. They fished two men to a boat; one managed the oars and the other the net. The canneries owned many of the boats. Each Sunday night during the fishing season a company tug with dozens of small boats in tow headed for the fishing grounds. The fishermen would be dropped off in their boats until the tug returned for them on Friday afternoon.

During that time they slept under a tarp at night and survived on hardtack, bacon and eggs and coffee cooked on a cut-down coal-oil can.

The men worked for independent contractors and were paid for their catch by the fish or by the pound. Most fishermen purchased their supplies at the cannery store, so companies often paid the fishermen with tokens instead of cash, then tripled the prices in their company store, knowing the fisherman had no choice but to buy from them.

In 1912, the W.E. Anderson cannery at Quathiaski Cove issued tokens in eight denominations, worth from one to a hundred fish. Most of the fishermen were Kwakiutl from Cape Mudge. Seeing how they were

Louise Hansen and I (front row left) were among the cannery workers at the Canadian Fishing cannery at Goose Bay in the late 1940s.

being cheated, their chief, Billy Assu, kept the fishing fleet tied up in protest. Eventually the Indians forced the company to discontinue the use of tokens.

In time, the gillnetter skiffs began to use gasoline engines, and power winches eased the back-breaking labour of hauling the gillnets over the roller at the stern of the boat. Developed by the Finnish fishermen of Sointula, the drum method of gillnetting and seining increased productivity ten times. Other technological innovations caused changes in the fishing industry. By 1910, cold storage plants were built in Vancouver and Prince Rupert (which became the terminus of the Grand Trunk Railway in 1913). This increased the market for fresh frozen fish, including salmon, cod and halibut.

Nanaimo and Barkley Sound were the original centres for herring fishing in British Columbia. The fishermen used purse seines and had boats three times the size of the original gillnetters. There was a lot of waste, and tons of herring were put through a reduction plant and turned into fertilizer. During the 1930s, the Japanese, who made up a large part of the BC fishing fleet, built herring salteries and exported to China and Japan.

Long-lining from dories was the most common method used to catch halibut and other ground fish during the first part of this century. Even today in the more remote areas you will hear the expression, "He's a long-liner." Today most of them have larger boats with engines, but long-lining is still a way to subsist without investing a lot of money.

Trolling for salmon was introduced during the early days of this century and has remained the most popular method of harvesting spring and coho salmon. Trolling vessels vary in size. Those used during the first half of the century were usually in the thirty-foot range, making it possible for an average person to buy a boat and gear. If trollers needed financing, they approached a fishing company

Below: Canadian Fishing Company cannery at Goose Bay, Rivers Inlet, 1949.

like Nelson Brothers, agreeing to sell fish to the company that financed them until their debt was paid.

In 1916, there were about 500 trolling boats

Below: Working a machine that put on lids in a salmon cannery. (BCARS 75289)

A tidal pool with seaweed, on a rock where small fish and crabs wait for the sea to return. An evergreen tree casts intricate reflections.

registered. Today they number in the thousands. During the first half of the century, the fishing companies had stations in strategic locations where the trollers could sell their fish. A fish-packing vessel transported the salmon from the station to a freezing plant or major centre. In the early days a troller was only large enough to carry ice for three or four days. Today the trolling industry is more sophisticated; the boats are larger, they travel much farther offshore, and they either have an ice machine aboard or they can carry enough ice to stay on the fishing grounds for several weeks.

The tradition of the troller is an individual one, and the troller looks on himself as the aristocrat of the fishing trade in British Columbia. My brother-in-law, Bill Olsen from New Westminster, who married my eldest sister Edith, trolled off this coast for forty-five years. For him it was a way of life. During the season he worked long, hard hours and was always one of the top boats. His boats—first the *Crown* and then the *Heritage*—were always spotlessly clean.

The decline in fishing stocks, and the concentration of fish processing and canning into larger units based in the lower mainland or Prince Rupert, removed an important source of income for the coastal villages, contributing to the decline in their population. The number of canneries on the coast has dropped from ninety-four in 1917 to the fourteen that are still in operation. During the past fifty years, seventy-three canning companies have come and gone.

Over the years, many other changes have taken place along our coast. Advances in transport and communications and the technology of the resource industry have changed the pattern of coastal settlement. Some villages have grown. Others have disappeared.

2. Lund

Lund is a small village located about a hundred miles north of Vancouver on the Malaspina Peninsula. Sheltered by Seville Island to the north and by an outcropping of bluffs and a forest to the east, it was once a main fuel stop and supply centre on the coast. Long before the turn of the century, there were a general store, post office, licensed hotel — and a wharf with piped-in fresh water.

Many people played a part in Lund's early history, but it was the brothers Charles and Fred Thulin who laid the foundation on which the village grew. Charles was the first to arrive. In 1886, he came to Vancouver from Sweden and booked into Pete Larsen's Union Hotel in Gastown. He was a husky young twenty-three-year old with a vision of the future and the confidence that in Canada, with a little work, an ordinary man could live like a king.

Before long he discovered that the swinging town of Gastown, with bars on every corner, was not the place he had dreamed of living. In his broken English, Charles began inquiring about other parts of the coast. A tugboat skipper told him: "There's a place called Desolation Sound about a hundred miles to the north. The weather is good up there. Get a boat and have a look for yourself."

With only a few dollars in his pocket, he asked around and was told where he could

find a clinker-built rowboat near the Indian village in English Bay. It was in need of repair with a few planks missing, but nothing so bad that a skilled craftsman like Charles Thulin couldn't fix it. Within a week, the boat was back in the water waiting to go north.

A few days later, in the wake of a southeasterly gale, with the chill of the damp air in his bones, he began his journey north in search of a homestead. His supplies were meagre, including basic provisions, tools, map, bedroll,

The village of Lund celebrated its 100th birthday in the summer of 1989.

Lund, seen here in 1954, is spread out around the new hotel. The machine shop and boatyard are to the left of the hotel.

Early pioneers like Charles Thulin headed north up the coast in small open boats. (BCARS 72568)

tarp and a makeshift sail that he used when the wind was fair. Otherwise he rowed. Wind and rain prevailed most of the time, but Charles Thulin persevered. He explored the bays and inlets along the coast for many weeks. The ocean was filled with fish and waterfowl and, using a hook and line with string as a lure, he could catch a cod within minutes. At night, after bailing out the seawater and

rainwater from the bottom of his boat, he tied the tarp over the gunwales and, still in his oilskins, pulled the damp bedding over his tired body and lay down to rest. The next day, if the skies were clear and the wind fair, he tied the bedding to the rigging to dry. On a good day, he averaged twenty miles. When the weather was stormy, he explored the land on foot.

Thulin arrived in late spring at what is now

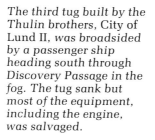

The third tug built by the Thulin brothers, City of Lund II, *was broadsided by a passenger ship heading south through Discovery Passage in the fog. The tug sank but most of the equipment, including the engine, was salvaged.*

Powell River. There he spent several weeks looking around. His next stop was Sliammon, the Indian village to the north. He enjoyed the company of the native Indians. They certainly didn't speak Swedish or Finnish, but he had no difficulty communicating.

Rowing north from Sliammon, Thulin came to a small bay sheltered by a rocky peninsula. A stream tumbled down over the rocks into the ocean and a dense forest stood close to shore. After pulling his boat onto the beach and tying it to a rock, he climbed the rocky bluff above the bay. A spectacular view of the Strait of Georgia and the offshore islands opened in front of him. As he sat looking over the ocean, he thought of the Swedish word "lund," meaning a tranquil place with shade trees and a stream. If this was to be his place, he would name it "Lund."

Charles Thulin spent a few days looking over the land, then rowed back to Vancouver to file claim for the 160-acre homestead. When his papers were in order, he returned to the coast. He stopped for a few days in Lund, then went hand-logging in Desolation Sound to earn money to pay for his brother Fred to come from Sweden. Working from first light until dark, Charles managed to sell enough logs in a year's time to pay Fred's passage.

Fred arrived on March 4, 1889. He was a strapping young man of sixteen, as fit as his brother and keen to start a new life in Canada. He also stayed at the Union Hotel, until he found passage to Desolation Sound. The boat he sailed on was the side-wheel steam tug SS *Mermaid*, hauling a barge loaded with slab wood to fire her boilers.

During the long hours working in the woods, Charles and Fred talked about building a fueling station at Lund for the wood-burning steam vessels travelling that part of the coast. They would sell the slab wood for fuel while they were clearing the land for their homestead. Toward the end of summer, they had sold enough logs to pay for the material to build a refuelling dock. They rowed to Vancouver and purchased spikes, chain and cable, as well as two oxen to haul the timber to the dock. Most of these supplies were delivered to Lund by tug and barge.

It was late in 1889 by the time they began building the dock. The winter rains, sleet and freezing temperatures had already begun. The two brothers persevered and by spring the following year, the wharf was completed. It was built on the south side of the bay where there was shelter from the winter gales and near the creek, which made it easier to pipe fresh water to the dock for the ships' boilers.

Some of the tugs coming from Vancouver carried mail, and Lund became known as "the place to get mail." As the fuel business flourished, the demand for provisions grew. Once again the brothers began building, this

Mr. and Mrs. A. Larson of Lund, standing on a giant fir taken from the forest on the Malaspina Peninsula.

time with lumber cut in their new sawmill. By 1892 both the store and post office were in operation. The post office was the only one on the coast north of Gibson's Landing.

By the time the store and post office were finished, the Union Steamship boats were calling twice a week with freight, mail and passengers. Lund became the hub of that part of the coast, with people rowing from many miles away to pick up their mail and supplies. These individuals, weary from rowing great distances in small open boats, often had to lay over for a day or two. This created a need for a hotel, and Charles and Fred went back to the drawing board. By the spring of 1894, the hotel at Lund was booking guests, and an open-air pavilion had been added to the central part of the store. There were always more people looking for accommodation than was available at the small hotel, so the brothers began building a larger one. It was named the Annex and went into operation the following year.

The Thulin brothers always had more than one project on the go. While they were building the wharf, store and hotels, their logging operation was in full swing. By this time they had a team of six oxen. Tree stumps were hauled out to clear the land for farming. Stumps too big for the oxen to move were set on fire and burned. Once the land was cleared the Thulins planted a garden and built shelters for chickens and other livestock. This was more than two men could handle, so they hired some settlers to give them a hand.

The brothers were also building boats. The first was a small gasoline-powered boat they used for catching dogfish. It was a great little boat, very seaworthy and designed after the ones used in the Baltic. The Thulins were adept craftsmen and by the turn of the century they had built and sold several small boats. One of the boats they built was a little tug to help with their logging business. Looking forward to the growth of their settlement, they

Finn Bay. Named after the Finnish settlers who moved there near the turn of the century, it is a popular anchorage for boaters when the Lund marina is full.

The Breakwater Inn, seen here in 1985, was built in 1910 and named the Malaspina Hotel. The name was changed in the 1960s. The building has been modernized somewhat, but much of the old charm remains.

optimistically named her the *City of Lund*. She was a lovely boat, powered by a small triple expansion steam engine, but she was destroyed by fire a year later. In 1903, they built the SS *Dolphin* to replace her.

Aside from their Lund operation, the brothers built stores on floats at Powell River and Sliammon. With energy left over and even some time, they began looking for a new area to develop. The obvious one was across the

Strait of Georgia at Campbell River on Vancouver Island. These plans were realized in March 1904, when Charles loaded a scow with a horse and buggy, lumber and other building equipment and towed it over to Campbell River with the *Dolphin*. There he built a wharf and fuelling station at the mouth of the river. When that project was complete, he began construction of Campbell River's first hotel, the Willows, which was open for business on July 1 that same year.

Many of the pioneers who settled near Lund were of Swedish or Finnish descent. For the next thirty years, their family names were synonymous with the growth of the region. Familiar names included Korpi, Hanson, Mietenen, Pitkanen, Simonson, Hendrickson, Franzen, Koshi, Lokenen, Opanos, Larson, Rasmussen, Salo, and Sorensen. There were also a few non-Scandinavian names, such as Buchanan, Hurley, Osborne, Pryor, Newman and West. Many of the Finlanders settled in the bay to the north of Lund, now known as Finn Bay.

Frank Osborne was one of the early settlers in Lund. Frank was from the eastern United States. He arrived on the coast in 1901 and first saw Lund when he was heading north to fish salmon in Rivers Inlet. He went back to Lund in 1905 and opened a machine shop. Jim Spilsbury, who grew up nearby on Savary Island and knew Frank well, describes him as one of the world's natural geniuses. In Jim's

words: "He was one of the most unforgettable people I've ever met. He was tall with a hooked nose and spoke few words. He was naturally dark and even blacker when covered with grease and soot from his shop." Frank Osborne had little formal education but for years he built and sold his own marine engines. He turned out the parts on his lathe, and had a foundry for casting the cylinders. He sold two models, the F.R. Osborne single cylinder heavy-duty, and the F.R. Osborne two cylinder heavy-duty. At that time Frank had the only machine shop on the coast north of Vancouver.

By 1907, Lund had a one-room school for the first eight grades. In those days it was necessary to have ten school-aged children registered to qualify for a teacher. This number was difficult to achieve, as many of the people on the coast in the early days were bachelors. As a result, the most welcome settlers were those with children. When Axel and Marie Hanson moved to Lund from Michigan in 1907 with their daughters Helen and Leana, there were enough children to open a school. Helen was only five years old at the time, but they needed her to get a teacher, so she got permission to start early.

The Hanson family later moved to Galley Bay, but the girls continued to attend the Lund School, spending weekdays in Lund and weekends at home. This was far safer than trying to commute during the winter months.

Helen recalled a boating accident that claimed the life of Mrs. Simpson, a teacher at the school, in 1912. "They had closed the school because of a severe snowstorm. I remember the day well as we were sleigh riding when we were shocked by the news. They had found the small boat full of water that Mrs. Simpson and some friends were taking to Powell River. The bodies were never recovered." In 1912, the road to Powell River ended four miles

Helen Anderson's home on Seville Island in 1984; Lund in the background.

Some of the old houses are still located along the boardwalk near the water.

Above: Helen Hanson Anderson's daughter, Violet, taking her dog for a row, 1927.

Right: Linea Hanson and George Vaughan, standing; (left to right) Kay Hanson, Bessie Vaughan, Violet Anderson and Pete Anderson.

Right: Violet Anderson (at left) and Elsa Balry feeding the chickens at the Anderson homestead at Turner Bay.

south of where Craig Road now meets the Lund highway. It was not completed until 1924.

In 1909, the Thulin brothers built another tug, also named the *City of Lund*. By then Fred had a Master's ticket for both passenger and towing vessels, and he skippered the tug himself whenever he had time.

In 1911, a new hotel was completed after five years of construction. It was named the Malaspina, after the peninsula on which it was located. With some minor changes, it is the same hotel still standing in Lund today. The new building was a treat to the eye, with well-kept gardens and honeysuckle and climbing roses enhancing the entrance. On the first floor there was a lounge, two large dining rooms, a kitchen and a pub. On the second floor were bedrooms and four bathrooms. In the summer months the rooms were filled with guests who had come to Lund aboard the Union Steamship vessel SS *Cassiar*.

Following World War I, a number of new settlers came to Lund, among them the Peter Sorensen family from Denmark. Peter's son Jens, a talented machinist, went to work for Frank Osborne. When Frank retired many years later, Jens took over the shop. Jens died in 1980 and his two sons are now in charge of the Lund Machine Shop.

In 1920, the *City of Lund* sank in an accident. She was tied alongside a log boom at Duncan Bay, in Discovery Passage, when the passenger ship SS *Admiral Evans*, southbound in the fog, hit her broadside and cut her in half. The *Admiral Evans* backed off and continued on course, leaving Clarence Thulin, one of Fred's sons, and another crew member waving frantically on the log boom. The *City of Lund* sank in shallow water. The engine and most of the equipment were saved and installed on the SS *Niluth*, built a couple of years later.

These were unlucky times for the Thulin

family. About the same time the second *City of Lund* sank, the Annex caught fire and burned to the ground. Jim Spilsbury recalls seeing the fire from Savary Island. "Why the Malaspina Hotel didn't burn down a thousand times is a miracle. As there was no central heating in the hotel, drum heaters were installed to keep the rooms warm and for the tenants to cook on. The smokestacks stuck out the windows with a steady stream of sparks coming from them!"

The Malaspina Hotel survived and continued to be the hot spot on the coast for many years. Dances held at the hotel were some of the best, with music often supplied by local people. "The Savary Island Trio" was one of the musical groups that played. The trio included Jim Spilsbury on drums, Alan May on clarinet, and Alice Marlett on piano, all residents of the island. Spilsbury recalls the time they were invited to play for a Christmas party at the Malaspina. "It was freezing cold, but that was all part of the fun. So with the exception of the piano, we loaded the instruments into a small open boat and with the engine running at full throttle we made a dash for Lund. I'll never forget that party. They were mostly Swedes and Finns dancing like feathers and in spite of it the whole building shook. To top it off, in the middle of the party water began pouring down in the middle of the dance floor, but people just laughed and continued to dance." The water was coming from the plumbing pipes, which had frozen and burst.

Berthe and Vine Miettenen relax in their rowboat in front of their home in Finn Bay.

In 1927, the Thulin brothers ended their partnership. Charles took over the Campbell River holdings and resided there until he died in 1932. Fred stayed in Lund until his death in 1935. Management of the Lund properties was taken over by Gerald and Holger Thulin, Fred's sons by his second marriage. Fred's marriage to May Palmer of Theodosia Arm had

Fred (at left) and Charles Thulin, the brothers who founded the village of Lund in the late 1880s.

"The Four Aces" dance band at Powell River with Dr. Charles Gould (front left), a well-known ocean sailor, playing saxophone, 1920s.

ended in divorce, and he had married Ida Wainio in 1911. He had three sons by his first marriage — Oscar, Clarence and Harold — and two sons, Gerald and Holger, by his second, as well as one daughter, Ethel, who died as a young woman.

Gerald married Ruby Korpi, who had grown up on the Korpi farm just outside Lund. They ran the store and the post office. Holger, who married Grace Randall, ran the hotel dining rooms and pub.

The operation at Lund prospered until the 1950s, when a series of misfortunes took their toll. The first was in 1952, when a severe westerly storm hit Lund and destroyed the wharf. The wharf was rebuilt the following year, but shortly afterwards, Holger died. The much-needed government dock and breakwater were built in 1956, but bad luck continued and a big new store that was constructed near the dock was destroyed by fire the next year.

The two families continued the operation until 1961, when, after seventy-five years in business, they sold to new owners. Thulin Passage, separating the Copeland Islands from the mainland north of Lund, is named after these distinguished pioneers.

Some members of the early settler families still live in Lund. Helen Anderson (nee Han-son), who has spent most of her life in logging camps and fishing with her husband, moved back in 1963 and until recently was living on Seville Island at the mouth of Finn Bay. When I saw her a couple of years ago, she was in her eighties and had the vitality of a young girl. She was still routinely running her outboard over to Lund.

In August 1989, the village of Lund celebrated its 100th anniversary. The SS *Niluth*, built by Charles and Fred Thulin in 1922, travelled to Lund to take part in the celebrations. The *Niluth* is now the *Viking* and is owned by Ken and Dorothy Mackenzie, who have restored her as a yacht.

The village is still very charming. Some of the original boardwalk still skirts the bay, and some of the old-timers and old houses are still around. The hotel, recently renamed the Lund Breakwater Inn, still does a good business during the summer months. There is a store and a fuel dock, and the first-class Sorensen boatyard and machine shop, originally owned by Frank Osborne.

Set on the Malaspina Peninsula, just around the corner from Desolation Sound, Lund was once a major coastal port. Now it is a pleasant stopover for visitors that retains much of the flavour of its pioneer history.

3. The Wishbone

About one hundred miles north of Vancouver, near the southwest entrance to Desolation Sound, a body of water shaped like a wishbone makes up Malaspina, Lancelot, Okeover and Theodosia inlets. It is a scenic wonderland where small bays and fjords are sheltered by the Malaspina and Gifford peninsulas, and set against a backdrop of mountainous peaks that extend as far as the eye can see.

Boaters enter this almost landlocked sea at the mouth of Malaspina Inlet, then follow a rocky channel for about three miles into Okeover and Lancelot inlets. At this point, the channel widens and deepens with average depths midstream between ten and fifty feet. In Theodosia Inlet the waters are shallow and one must navigate with extreme care. In the inner arms of The Wishbone there is little tidal flow; water temperatures there remain higher than in most parts of the coast.

To the Europeans who first settled on the coast, discovering the protected waters and fertile lands surrounding these inlets was like finding Shangri-la. It was a paradise, where wild animals roamed freely through grass-

Laura Cove off Prideaux Haven is one of the wonderful small boat anchorages in Desolation Sound.

Aerial view of Bliss Landing, a picturesque cove on the Malaspina Peninsula. Once a place where locals socialized, it is now a private club for members only. (George McNutt photo)

Above: Joe Copeland (at left) standing on the verandah of his house in Portage Cove with Louie Anderson, the husband of Irene Palmer from the Palmer ranch, 1918.

Far right (left to right): Helen Anderson, her father Axel Hanson, her daughter Violet and a friend, Teddy Ricka, in Galley Bay, 1923.

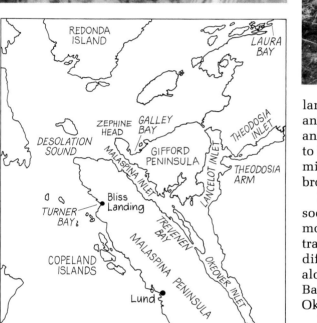

Helen Gidloff and her daughter enjoy an evening row in Theodosia Arm, 1916.

lands and mountain slopes, and the beaches and waters were inhabited by numerous birds and other sea life. Stately timbers grew down to the water's edge, and only the distant drumming of a grouse or the lonely cry of a loon broke the silence.

Little wonder almost every secluded bay soon had someone living on it! They were mostly bachelors who hand-logged and trapped for a living, recluses who were difficult to get along with and chose to be alone. Joe Copeland, who settled in Trevenen Bay where it was just a short portage into Okeover Arm, was an example.

Like the others, Joe was a loner. He was seldom seen without his Luger pistol and the

grey uniform of the Confederate States. When he wasn't chewing tobacco or spitting snuff, he talked about his past, mostly about the Civil War when he had served as a bugler fighting for the South. His father had fought on the other side. When the war ended, Joe escaped to Canada. He arrived in Gastown, outfitted a small rowboat with oars and sails, packed his few belongings and rowed north along the coast to make his fortune. He spent most of his time around Desolation Sound, where he logged, trapped and bartered with the Indians. The Ragged Islands north of Lund had their name changed to the Copeland Islands, in memory of this "old-timer."

The Palmer family moved to Canada from Oregon in the late 1860s, about the same time as Joe Copeland came. They settled near the Trent River on Vancouver Island, where they farmed and raised their five children (two girls and three boys) before moving to the section of land between Grail and Galahad Points at the northern entrance to Theodosia Inlet. Most of the children were adults by the time their parents made the move.

The Palmer brothers, Banny, Al and Bill, formed the Palmer Owen logging company, a successful operation active on the coast for many years. It was a good-sized camp with more than sixty-five men on the payroll. Al Palmer, the middle son, was the boss. Like most logging operations of its size, Palmer Owen had several claims that it worked in rotation, moving from one to the other by water. As operations were completed on one claim, the equipment and buildings were skidded onto floats, and a tug would tow everything to the next claim.

One of the company's logging claims was in Theodosia Inlet, on land that was part of the parents' homestead. It was a good stand of tim-

ber, and falling the trees helped clear land for farming and raising cattle. Jim Spilsbury, who grew up on Savary Island, went to work for $3.20 a day for Palmer Owen when he was still a teenager. At first Jim worked as a woodbuck, using a long cross-cut saw to cut the blocks, then an axe to cut them into smaller pieces for firing the donkey engine. The donkey used about a cord and a half of wood a day. During the first part of the century, most of the engines were operated by steam, and it took a crew of four—a woodbuck, a woodsplitter, a fireman and an engineer—to keep them running.

Meanwhile, the senior Palmers settled on their homestead at the mouth of Theodosia Inlet. They built fences and cultivated the land for farming. When the grass was growing and the barns and stalls were built, they brought in a herd of beef and dairy cattle. The Palmer farm soon became the main supplier of

The Oscar Roos family, Lancelot Inlet.

Ed Burglund and his boat on the beach in Theodosia Inlet. Burglund was one of the early settlers in The Wishbone.

Running a steam donkey in Turner Bay in the 1920s. The Copeland Islands are in the background.

beef and farm produce for the Thulin brothers' store at Lund and for logging operations on that part of the coast. In order to transport produce and bring in supplies, the settlers got together and built a rough road between Okeover Inlet and Lund. This saved the Palmers the long haul around Sarah Point and down the outside of the Malaspina Peninsula to Lund.

Pa Palmer had a greater appetite for peace and solitude than most men, so when the fall harvest was over he left the homestead to his wife, Sarah, and rowed in a small open boat to the head of Bute Inlet. Then, with his packsack, an axe and other survival gear, he hiked up past the Waddington Canyon. Winter after winter he made his home in this mountain retreat, taking shelter in a lean-to shack he had built on his first visit, and living mainly on the

wild animals he caught in his trapline. He lived to a ripe old age, but when he died, his family claimed that he had drunk too much glacial water and that the sediment in the water had killed him.

May Palmer, the eldest of the Palmer girls, had moved to Theodosia with her parents. Near the turn of the century, she met and married Fred Thulin from Lund. The younger of their two sons, Clarence, is still living in Campbell River. When May's marriage to Fred ended in divorce a few years later, she married Charlie Salo, one of the settlers from Finn Bay. After their marriage, Charlie took over the management of the Palmer farm, doing the heavy work and delivering supplies.

The Gifford Peninsula protects The Wishbone from the north and easterly winds. Zephine Head, which forms the northern tip of the

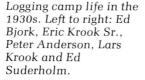

Logging camp life in the 1930s. Left to right: Ed Bjork, Eric Krook Sr., Peter Anderson, Lars Krook and Ed Suderholm.

peninsula, curves to the east and shelters a large basin of water named Galley Bay. The bay, pre-empted by Axel Hanson in 1907, was a fertile section of land with good timber, and the Hansons had a combined logging and farming operation there for many years. It was while they were living in Galley Bay that their two daughters, Helen and Leana, took board and room at Lund to attend school.

When I visited with Helen in her home on Seville Island, she showed me pictures and talked about their life on the homestead in Galley Bay. "There was always plenty to do. I used to help my mother look after the animals, feed the chickens and milk the cows. There was time for fun, too, and my dog and I would go rowing, sometimes just drifting along in the bay." Helen married Peter Anderson, and they spent many happy years together logging and fishing. After his death, Helen stayed on in their home on Seville Island overlooking Finn Bay.

In the 1960s, another kind of coastal settler took over the land and vacant buildings in Galley Bay. It was the time of communes, and the Galley Bay commune was one of the largest on the coast, attracting young people from all over the continent. At times there were up to fifty adults and as many children living in little shacks and A-frames under the trees, and using the Hanson homestead as headquarters and communal dining room. Lack of a stable and dedicated core of members led to the breakup of the commune within a few years. The land has now returned to nature.

The inlets that form the arms of The Wishbone are now part of the Desolation Sound Marine Park, preserved as a wilderness area for everyone to enjoy. The old cattle trail between Okeover Inlet and Lund is now a paved road. Nailed to a post overlooking this beautiful part of the coast is a sign that reads: "This is the northern terminus of the Pan American highway that stretches 15,040 kilometres down the west coast of the Americas to Puerto Montt, Chile."

Above left: A day at the beach in Desolation Sound.

Above right: Boat Day at Bliss Landing on the Malaspina Peninsula. People gathered from farms and nearby villages to meet the Union Steamship boat to pick up mail and freight, and to exchange yarns and have a good time.

Looking across Okeover Inlet.

4. Campbell River

Campbell River on Vancouver Island lies about 130 miles north of Vancouver and marks the western entrance to Discovery Passage. The Cape Mudge lighthouse on southern Quadra Island, a guide to mariners since the turn of the century, can be seen blinking its warning on the opposite shore. This picturesque town is known all over the world for the giant chinook salmon caught in nearby waters. To local mariners, however, it is better known as the last major centre to take on supplies before heading north through Seymour Narrows and Johnstone Strait.

It is about an hour's run from Campbell River to Seymour Narrows, at a boat speed of nine knots. If possible, boaters head north on a high-water slack as the current in Johnstone Strait can run up to four knots. The northern

The Campbell River waterfront, with the Willows Hotel in the background, 1947. The hotel was built by Charles Thulin in 1904 and stayed in business until fire destroyed it in 1963.

edition of the tide tables is used from Campbell River north, as the tables are divided where the tidal systems meet. The ebb flows north through Discovery Passage and Johnstone Strait to the open Pacific at the northern end of Vancouver Island, and the flood flows south. This is opposite to the tidal system in the Strait of Georgia, which flows in through the Strait of Juan de Fuca at the southern end of the island. The meeting of the tidal systems creates a pocket in the water around Desolation Sound and helps keep the salt water warmer than on other parts of the coast.

Campbell River was named after Dr. Samuel Campbell, surgeon aboard the British survey ship HMS *Plumper*, which surveyed the Gulf of Georgia and the surrounding waters between 1857 and 1861. It was late autumn when the *Plumper* lay off the mouth of Campbell River and Dr. Campbell noted in his diary that the Kwakiutl people were already in residence in their winter village. He was impressed by the high rail fences that surrounded the village for protection from any enemy. In the summer, the Indians took apart their cedar-board houses and moved them inland to the Quinsam River flats, where they picked berries, hunted game and fished and smoked salmon for their winter food stores before moving back near the ocean at Campbell River.

An epidemic of measles and smallpox decimated the Campbell River Indians near the turn of the century. Survivors either joined the Cape Mudge band or moved to a smaller, poorer village at the "Spit." No longer poor, the Campbell River band today is now spearheading a marine development that includes a long-awaited docking facility for cruise ships.

At the turn of the century, Quathiaski Cove and Heriot Bay were the main centres in the area and few Europeans were living around Campbell River. It was not until Charles Thulin came over from Lund that the river mouth began attracting non-native settlers. Charles and his brother, Fred, had pioneered the village of Lund on the Malaspina Peninsula. They were the kind of people who worked hard and had a special insight into the needs of the people on the coast.

Charles arrived in Campbell River in the spring of 1904, aboard the *Dolphin*, one of the tugs built by the two brothers in Lund. The *Dolphin* was pulling a scow loaded with tools

and materials to begin building a wharf near the mouth of the Campbell River, similar to the one in Lund, where ships could take on fuel. The wharf was intended to be a government project, but when the funding got lost in the bureaucracy, Thulin went ahead on his own and finished it in record time by employing mainly Indians. Ships could now take on cordwood to fire their boilers, rather than hauling the wood in a scow behind them.

The wharf was a landmark for forty years. In spite of the fierce southeasterly winds that funnel down Discovery Passage, the only interruption in service occurred in 1917 when a storm blew down the landward piers. They were quickly rebuilt and service was resumed.

In 1958, Ripple Rock was destroyed with 1,375 tons of special explosives to make Seymour Narrows safer for navigation. Currents here can run more than fifteen knots.

The steamship USS Cardena heading through Seymour Narrows before Ripple Rock was destroyed. Note the current and whirlpools in the foreground.

Canadian Fishing Company cannery with a seiner moored alongside. Fisherman's Marina, Campbell River.

Checking the nets for damage and rolling them back on the drum at the marina, Campbell River, 1980s.

Once the wharf was built, Charles began work on a hotel. He was an old hand at this kind of construction, having worked with his brother Fred to build the Malaspina Hotel at Lund. On July 1, 1904, the Willows Hotel was open for business, with Emerson Hannan as its first manager. Along with the fame of the tyee salmon, the Willows Hotel became known all over the world. It catered to tourists, loggers, fishermen and prospectors, and its guest list also boasted the occasional celebrity, including Bob Hope and Bing Crosby. The hotel was

the social centre for that part of the coast, remaining in business until fire destroyed it in 1963.

The original general store, located near the hotel, was later replaced by a much larger store, the Campbell River Trading Company, at the entrance to the wharf. It was known as the "big store." Halmar Hagstrom, a partner of the Thulin brothers in Campbell River, managed the store and, in 1907, became the town's first postmaster.

The "big store" was sold to F.J. Cross in 1926 and operated under the name of Cross and Vanstone. The original store was moved back from the beach and converted into living quarters for Charles Thulin and his family. It later became a residential hotel known as Thulin Court.

The influence of the Thulin family in Campbell River was so strong that when the village was incorporated in 1947, two of the three elected commissioners were Thulins: Carl, son of Charles Thulin, and Oscar, the son of Frederick.

Doctors and hospitals were scarce on the coast during the first part of the century, and because logging was the number one industry, there were many serious accidents. The nearest hospital to Campbell River before 1914 was St. Michael's at Rock Bay, twenty-five miles north, near Chatham Point at the junction of Nodales Channel, Discovery Passage and Johnstone Strait. The strong tidal currents in Seymour Narrows just north of Campbell River often caused delays; many victims died before reaching hospital. Finally, in 1914, Campbell River got its own hospital. The land for the two-storey building was donated and cleared by the Thulins, and Howard Jamieson was the hospital's first doctor. The first baby born in the hospital was Mabel Wilson of Quathiaski Cove.

In 1922, a smallpox epidemic swept through the area. Since smallpox is such a highly contagious disease, it was necessary to burn all the mattresses in the hospital once the epidemic had subsided. With no money to replace them, the small facility was forced to close. It re-opened in 1926 as Our Lady of Lourdes, under the management of a religious order.

Logging and fishing are the prime industries on the coast, and the area around Campbell River has had its share of both. At Oyster Bay, just south of town, the open sweep of the Georgia Strait offers no protected waters for booming and sorting. When Al Simpson operated the Iron River Logging camp at Oyster Bay during the first half of the century, he overcame this problem by buying old ships from Seattle, both wood- and iron-hulled, to be towed in and sunk as a breakwater.

One luxuriously appointed four-master, the *St. Paul*, ended her colourful but melancholy history in Oyster Bay. It is ironic that a ship with such a holy name was built as a slaver just before the Civil War, but she made only a single trip in that capacity before slavery was outlawed in the United States. A succession of owners tried her in various trades—always just before the collapse of the market. She finally became a gambling ship off the California coast, but an onshore gale pushed her inside the three-mile limit and the Coast Guard confiscated her. The *St. Paul's* bad luck dogged her to her grave at Oyster Bay, where she sank too far out and at the wrong angle to stop the waves! Alas, her ill-fated timbers were washed away years ago. The area is now a provincial park site.

Campbell River salmon runs have been famous since the district was first settled. The coho run of 1921 was legendary: a Victoria paper reported that one man, with a "kicker" engine in a twelve-foot boat, caught 146 blueback in a single day. The fish taken near Campbell River are mainly chinook and coho, and ling cod and herring are also plentiful.

Commercial fishermen travel to where the fish are running. They go north to Prince Rupert or the Queen Charlottes in May, and come south as the season advances. As early as 1934, there were 150 gas boats and 180 rowboats engaged in trolling around Cape Mudge. During the height of the season, there are hundreds of commercial boats still fishing in Johnstone Strait.

Until recently, the only moorage available for holiday boaters in Campbell River was to raft alongside the outside vessel on the government float or at the nearby fishermen's marina. With the opening of the Discovery Harbour Marina in 1990, there is now moorage available for both commercial vessels and pleasure boats.

In 1958, Ripple Rock, a major obstacle to navigation in Seymour Narrows, was destroyed with 1,375 tons of special explosive, the world's largest non-atomic blast to that date. It was a major engineering achievement, undertaken to destroy a marine hazard that had destroyed at least twenty large and one hundred small vessels attempting to pass through the Narrows. On the day of the blast, Campbell River residents were warned to leave doors and windows open in case of shock waves. In fact, the town, nine miles away, was unaffected, as was a pod of five killer whales that passed only three miles from the explosion.

Campbell River has had disappointments. Until the Discovery Bay Marina opened, there was no adequate docking facility for ships, and most of the luxury cruise liners have continued to pass by. The Sitmar Lines' *Fairsea* collided with the Western Mines dock when she attempted to stop there in 1970, damaging the ship and the dock. Other ships stop in by accident. In July 1984, the luxury liner *Sun-*

dancer, on her maiden voyage, struck Maud Island in Seymour Narrows. She was beached in Duncan Bay, just north of Campbell River, where she lay on the shallow bottom until she was refloated and towed to Burrard Drydock in Vancouver. There she was declared a total loss and sold as scrap. But she was later repaired and sailed again for a new owner under a new name, *Pegasus*.

Air travel was pioneered in Campbell River by float planes, operated first in 1946 by BC Airlines Ltd. and then by Island Airlines, owned by the late Bob Langdon. Island Air stuck to coastal charter work throughout its life. Trained as a pilot in the RCAF, Langdon began flying "floats and boats" (float planes and flying boats) for BC Air shortly after World War II. He pioneered BC Air's base at Campbell River, and when the company

A seiner heading north in Discovery Passage, 1984. The pulp mill at Campbellton billows smoke in the background.

Looking across Discovery Passage to Quadra Island.

Looking south over the ferry dock at Campbell River and the fishermen's marina. (George McNutt photo)

changed ownership he started his own company.

Island Air's office and maintenance stores were located on a float in front of the Willows Hotel. For a time, the company had a fuelling station at Mansons Landing on Cortes Island.

Bob started with two aircraft in 1959, and had a fleet of twenty-three planes when he sold the company in 1977.

Improvements in communication have given Campbell River a third major industry: tourism. And the mainstay of tourism is sports

A grand, new Painters Lodge was built after fire destroyed the original building on Christmas Eve in 1985.

fishing for the tyee salmon (a chinook salmon weighing more than thirty pounds), of which the city is unarguably the world capital. Edward Painter pioneered the sports fishing industry at Campbell River. Born in England in 1887, he moved to Canada with his parents in 1896. They settled in Saskatchewan before moving west to British Columbia. Even as a boy Edward was interested in boats. His favourite toys were small wooden vessels he carved from scraps of wood. It was natural for him to become a boatbuilder, and when he was old enough he apprenticed as a shipwright in the Vancouver Shipyards. During World War I, he served as a shipwright, and he returned to BC after the war to open his own boatyard in Port Alberni.

Edward Painter married June Barclay, of the English banking family, in 1921. She was born at the turn of the century in Kelowna, and had met Edward in Port Alberni in 1920. They spent their first year of marriage in the mill town, where June remembers catching her first tyee. When the Painters moved to Campbell River in 1922, Edward went back into boatbuilding. He was a gifted craftsman and besides designing and building larger vessels, he designed a rowboat especially for fishing chinook. These sleek rowboats, fourteen feet long and three feet wide, became known as "tyee boats." The originals were clinker-built of yellow cedar, and weighed about seventy-five pounds before launching. About 200 of them were built, and their classic beauty and easy handling made them sought after around the world. They are still being produced, but now they are made of fibreglass.

Edward Painter and a group of distinguished international sports fishermen organized the Tyee Club at Campbell River in 1924. The objectives of the club were to:

1. Foster interest in Canada's greatest game fish.
2. Emphasize the ideals of sportsmanship as distinguished from slaughter.
3. Standardize fishing tackle and encourage young people in the craft of guiding.

In 1932, the Painters opened a resort. They started with a few small cabins; then, when demand for accommodation increased, they began construction of their famous lodge, completed in 1938. They sold the lodge in 1948 but continued in the sports fishing business on a smaller scale. Edward died in 1960, and his grandchildren still work as guides. In 1986, twenty-two-year-old Catherine Painter won the Tyee Man Trophy for the largest fish of the season when she landed a fifty-five-pound tyee in Discovery Passage.

Painters Lodge burned to the ground on Christmas Eve, 1985. It was rebuilt on a grander scale and once again plays host to sports fishermen from around the world. It faces April Point, an equally famous fishing resort on the other side of the passage, and there are dozens of other hotels, motels and campgrounds in the Campbell River area. They range from the large, deluxe Coast Discovery Inn in the town's main plaza to smaller, quieter resorts on the outskirts of town.

When I lived on the coast around Desolation Sound in the 1940s, Campbell River was still a village, but now it has all the amenities of a modern city. It is one of the most popular destinations in British Columbia, where people from all over the world come to visit.

5. Cape Mudge and Quathiaski Cove: The Native Influence

Cape Mudge marks the most southerly tip of Quadra Island. Rising 200 feet above sea level, this impressive headland also marks the southwest entrance to Discovery Passage. The high cliffs offer an unobstructed view of the large expanse of open water that makes up the northern part of Georgia Strait, and a superb vista of Wilby Shoals, the dangerous reef extending southward from Quadra where numerous ships have foundered.

Cape Mudge and Quathiaski Cove belonged to the Salish people when the first Europeans arrived. Quathiaski comes from *Qatasaken*, a Salish word meaning "a mouth with a bite of something in it." Grouse Island is the something in the bite.

In the summer of 1792, Captain Vancouver's two ships, the *Discovery* and the *Chatham*, arrived from Desolation Sound and anchored half a mile north of Cape Mudge, then moved on to the sheltered cove now known as Quathiaski. Vancouver and the ships' botanist, Archibald Menzies, went ashore at the cape and climbed the steep cliff to the Salish village called *Tsqulotn*, or "playing field."

That same year, Vancouver named the headland after his first lieutenant, Zachary Mudge. Lieutenant Mudge began his naval career in 1780 at the age of ten; by 1849 he had attained the rank of admiral. The island we know as Vancouver Island was originally named Quadra–Vancouver by Captains Quadra and Vancouver at their famous meeting at Nootka Sound in 1792. However, the British later eliminated the melodic Spanish names wherever possible and renamed British Columbia's largest island Vancouver. It was not until 1903 that Captain Quadra was honoured by having the second largest island on the coast named after him.

Archibald Menzies described the native settlement in his journal after his first trip ashore: "We found a considerable village consisting of about 12 Huts or houses planked over with large boards some of which were ornamented with rude paintings particularly on the fronts of the houses. They were flat roofed & of a quadrangular figure & each house contained several families to the number of about 350 inhabitants on the most moderate calculation."

He went on to describe the inhabitants: "Their hair is straight black and long but mixed with such quantity of red-ochre grease and dirt puffed over at times with down that the color is not easily distinguishable. Many of the men went entirely naked without giving the least offense to the other Sex or showing any apparent shame of their situation, they

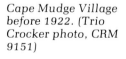

Cape Mudge Village before 1922. (Trio Crocker photo, CRM 9151)

have long black beards with long hair about their private parts but none on their Breasts or Arm pits. Some had ornamented their faces by painting it with red-ochre sprinkled with glitter which helped not a little to heighten their ferocious appearance.

"The women were decently covered with garments made either of the skins of wild animals or wove from wood or prepared bark of the American Arbor Vitae tree. Women and children did not appear anywise shy or timorous tho we were pretty certain our party were the first Europeans they had ever seen or had any direct intercourse with. Nor did they regard us or the Vessels with any degree of curiosity."

The Indians of Tsqulotn did not realize it, but their first encounter with Captain Vancouver and his men was the beginning of the end of their way of life. European explorers and settlers brought alcohol, sickness and guns which they distributed freely among the natives. The Indians had no tolerance for alcohol and were unable to resist European diseases such as measles and smallpox. The people who survived were placed on reserves; their land and status were taken from them and their ancient customs eroded.

Even before Europeans settled the coast, however, the Salish inhabitants of Tsqulotn were dispossessed by the fierce Lekwiltok branch of the southern Kwakiutl. In the mid-nineteenth century, already armed with guns from the traders, the Lekwiltok swept south from Johnstone Strait in their big war canoes. The clifftop village was never taken or burned by the invaders, but the Lekwiltok simply built their own village, Yaculta, on flat shoreland at the base of the cliff. Thus threatened, the people of Tsqulotn evacuated and joined the Salish villages around Comox.

The Yacultas, as the tribe was called, became a terror to the Salish as far down the coast as the Fraser River. They even tried to levy a toll on European vessels navigating Discovery Passage, which brought disciplinary visits from British gunboats. Drink and disease, as well as British guns, sapped the Yacultas' strength, and by the latter part of the nineteenth century, they had acquiesced to the jurisdiction of the Crown and life under the reserve system.

Indian reserves were administered by the federal Department of Indian Affairs, and the local Indian agent represented the government and its laws on each reserve. One agent sometimes had responsibility for a huge territory covering several reserves. Considering the great gulf between European and native cultures, the position of the Indian agent was an unenviable one. He had to interpret and enforce regulations made by bureaucrats thousands of miles away, for a suspicious population whose culture he only dimly understood. It is remarkable how many of these agents gained the acceptance, and even the respect, of the Indians.

One of the first Indian agents on Quadra

This photograph of a Kwakiutl bridal party, by the eminent American photographer Edward S. Curtis, conveys the fierce pride of the Kwakiutl people who occupied southern Quadra Island in the middle of the nineteenth century.

Logan and Gunhilde (at left) Schibler, a founding family of Owen Bay, in the late 1930s, waiting beneath a totem pole for the Union Steamship boat at Quathiaski Cove, with Mrs. Greenberg, a friend from Oregon.

A federal Department of Fisheries inspector examines a native dugout canoe under construction. (Department of Fisheries photo)

was Reginald H. Pidcock, who had pre-empted land in Quathiaski Cove in 1882, and was appointed Indian agent in 1886. He was stationed at Alert Bay, and from there he was expected to travel the coast by dugout canoe to visit the many Indian villages and reserves under his jurisdiction. Not surprisingly, his favourite visit was to Quathiaski, where he could camp on his own land.

Pidcock was a deeply religious man from a long line of Anglican clergymen. He had been attracted to Canada by the Cariboo Gold Rush, but never got to the gold fields. Instead, he homesteaded land in what is now the town of Courtenay. He pitched his tent in the woods and built a sawmill to cut logs for his house and a church. When the church was built, he carved a pulpit and reading desk for it. Decorations for the services were wildflowers and ferns gathered from the hills. Pidcock read the lessons by the flickering light of candles or oil lamps. Sometimes the entire congregation consisted of Pidcock's growing family.

Pidcock was a strong believer in education as well as religion, and he was responsible for the founding of Indian residential schools at Alert Bay and Quathiaski. Both institutions opened in 1894.

One of Pidcock's major difficulties as Indian agent was trying to enforce the Potlatch Law passed in 1884. The potlatch was an important social ceremony that confirmed status and traditional privileges and names among the coastal natives. A potlatch was celebrated with dancing, speeches and the distribution of personal property to invited guests. Many government officials and missionaries considered potlatching to be a waste of time and a cause of improvidence among the natives. The new law made attendance at potlatches a misdemeanor punishable by two to six months in prison.

As a devout Christian, Pidcock was dedicated to enforcing the anti-potlatch law. He wrote Ottawa: "It is quite certain that as long as this most demoralizing custom prevails, little or nothing can be done for the good of the Indians." However, he found that "the determination with which they cling to the custom, makes me think the opposition at first will be very strong." Pidcock pleaded for a jail, a white constable and local assistants, otherwise he could not carry out the law.

None of the Indian agents on the coast received these aids to enforcement, and the Indians mocked the new law as being "weak as a baby." Then, in 1889, Provincial Chief Justice Sir Matthew Begbie torpedoed Pidcock's attempt to convict a Kwakiutl named Hamasack for calling together a potlatch. Because of the vagueness of what the word potlatch signified, concluded Begbie, "it would be difficult, and probably impossible, to sustain a conviction under this statute."

For over twenty years, the Begbie decision effectively made the law a dead letter. Indian Affairs Superintendent Arthur Vowell told Indian agents in British Columbia to operate "under a policy of patience and moral suasion rather than coercion."

Chief Billy Assu of Cape Mudge had an outstanding record as a potlatcher during this period. He gave hundreds of potlatches. When he became chief, he entertained more than 2,000 guests from twenty-three tribes. The party lasted for two weeks, during which time he gave away $25,000 worth of gifts and food. On another occasion, Assu built a chief's Big

Quathiaski Cove as it is today.

House with two houseposts carved by Johnny Kla-wat-chi of Alert Bay. For the opening of the Big House, he invited all the chiefs of the Southern Kwakiutl nation to a potlatch.

However, the official attitude in Ottawa changed during the more militant atmosphere of World War I. Since the courts and the regular legal system had found the potlatch law unenforceable, in 1918 the Indian Affairs Department had Parliament pass an amendment to the Act giving Indian agents the powers of a Justice of the Peace to convict and sentence offenders against the potlatch law.

As a result, in the years immediately following the war, there was an increase in convictions under the law, especially in the Alert Bay district where the Kwakiutl were concentrated. The local agent was William Halliday, who had succeeded Pidcock and carried on Pidcock's tradition of strong opposition to the potlatch. The climax of Halliday's campaign came at the famous "Christmas Potlatch" held by Nimpkish chief Dan Cranmer on Village Island. Many thousands of dollars in gifts were distributed to 300 guests in a five-day ceremony. Participants considered it the biggest potlatch yet.

With the help of undercover witnesses coordinated by the RCMP, twenty-eight men and six women were arrested and charged with potlatching, among them Chief Billy Assu of the Cape Mudge Lekwiltok. The trial began February 27, 1922 before William Halliday, who shared the bench with A.W. Wastell of Alert Bay. In consideration of Halliday's new powers, the Indians' defence attorney, W. Murray, entered guilty pleas and negotiated a complicated agreement binding the Kwakiutl

to refrain from potlatching and to surrender all potlatch regalia, which was given to the National Museum in Ottawa. Nearly all of the 300 guests at the potlatch signed the document, though a group of twenty-two participants, mainly from Fort Rupert, refused and received sentences of from two to six months in Oakalla.

Chief Billy Assu's agreement to end the potlatch system had a great influence over the southern Kwakiutl. In fact, even before the Christmas Potlatch, he called the people of Cape Mudge together and suggested they use the money from village logging enterprises to modernize the village, bring in electricity and water and pull down the old potlatch houses.

The potlatch amendment was removed from the Indian Act in 1951, too late to make a difference for most Indians, who had already forgotten their ancient songs and ceremonies.

The bold shoreline of southern Quadra Island.

The United Church at Cape Mudge Village.

Chief Billy Assu, who had given up potlatching in 1922, had worked hard toward this goal. In 1937, he was awarded a Coronation Medal by King George VI, and in 1953 he received a medal "for meritorious service" from Queen Elizabeth II.

His son, Harry, also has received a unique recognition. The Canadian five-dollar bill was engraved from a photo of Harry Assu's seiner taken during the great sockeye run of 1958. The *B.C.P. 45* was shown making a net set at Ripple Point, Campbell River. In the background is the seiner *Bruce Luck*, skippered by Don Assu.

Above: Carved mortuary figure stands guard outside the Kwagiulth Museum at Cape Mudge. The museum, opened in 1979, contains most of the unique Kwakiutl tribal regalia and coppers returned by the federal government after being confiscated following the 1921 "Christmas Tree" Potlatch.

Right: Cape Mudge Village stretches along the shoreline of southern Quadra Island.

Through the efforts of Chief Jimmy Sewid of Alert Bay and other members of the Kwakiutl nation, a portion of the regalia seized by the government was returned by the National Museum half a century after its confiscation. It is now housed at the Kwagiulth Museum opened at Cape Mudge in 1979. The opening was marked by a huge potlatch given by Chiefs Sewid, Harry Assu, and Jimmy Wilson of Kingcome Inlet, to dedicate the museum's twenty-nine-foot totem pole carved in memory of Chief Billy Assu. There were dances, and 1,500 pounds of barbecued salmon were supplied free to the hundreds of guests.

Cape Mudge village has a tradition of leadership in native rights issues. It was the Kwakiutl of the Cape Mudge Reserve who lodged a formal complaint that they paid taxes but were denied a vote in provincial elections. The protest was supported by the major native Indian organizations, the Pacific Coast Native Fishermen's Union, and the Native Brotherhood of British Columbia. In 1949, when British Columbia granted Indians the vote, William Scow of Alert Bay and Chief Assu's son Frank went together to Victoria to thank the legislative assembly.

The Cape Mudge village was the first native Indian village in Canada to seek municipal status. The land includes the lighthouse property, which is leased back to the government, as well as acreage at Village Bay, Open Bay, Drew Harbour and on Vancouver Island.

Above right: Cape Mudge lighthouse, one of the few manned lighthouses remaining on the coast. Stormy waters off the Cape have claimed over 200 vessels since the first light was erected in 1898.

Right: A bait boat distributes live bait to sports fishermen.

6. Quadra Island: European Influence

Many of the families living on southern Quadra Island today trace their roots back to the early days of settlement, and the roads that link their villages are the logging roads of yesterday. Some of the villages, such as Granite Bay, no longer exist. Other locations, such as the row of waterfront shacks called "Poverty Point," have developed a more prosperous ambience.

William R. Clark was the first European to purchase land on southern Quadra. In May 1882, he bought 144 acres in Gowlland Harbour. Soon after, Indian agent R.H. Pidcock purchased 167 acres of land at Quathiaski Cove. Both Pidcock and Clark later transferred their acreages to William Sayward, owner of a sawmill in Victoria. Sayward himself purchased large areas of land on Quadra, as did Moses Ireland, an independant logger and timber buyer.

The 1887 *British Columbia Yearbook* described Quadra as one of the principal timber locations in the province. Within a year of Clark's purchase, most of the big timber leases on the island had been taken over by large companies like Merrill Lumber Company of Seattle, Moodyville Sawmill Company and Royal City Planing Mills Company.

In the late 1880s, logging camps on southern Quadra included Hiram McCormick in Hyacinthe Bay and King & Casey in Quathiaski Cove. The Hasting Sawmill Company, one of the bigger operations at the time, was logging

This row of shacks was known as "Poverty Point" in the early 1940s. The shacks were the beginning of the now-famous April Point Lodge.

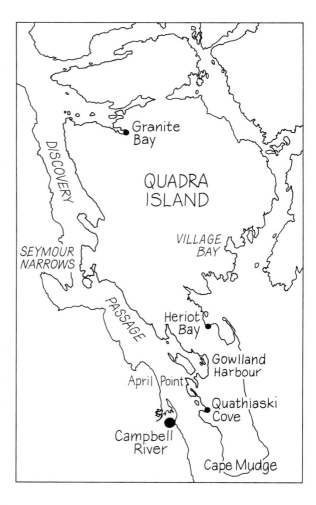

farther up the west side of the island in Granite Bay. Logging also went on in the central part of the island near Village and Main lakes. The Moffat brothers built a dam there to raise the water level so that a tug could tow the logs to the southern end of Village Lake. From there they entered a long flume, which brought them into Village Bay. The route is still indicated by the name "flume trail" on local maps.

Native inhabitants were of two minds about lumbering. On the one hand, they saw their land being taken away from them, and some even tried to retaliate by setting fire to the "witness trees" that marked out the timber claims. On the other hand, they realized there was no chance of stopping the new industry. Instead of resisting, many sought logging rights for themselves. Indian agent R.H. Pidcock gave permission to the Cape Mudge Band to cut timber on its reserve for sawlogs. The Indians also got permission to extract oil from

dogfish, which they sold to the logging camps for skid-grease, a profitable cash business.

By the turn of the twentieth century, before Campbell River had begun to develop, settlement on southern Quadra was thriving. There were lumber camps, mills, two post offices, a hotel, a Methodist mission, an all-white public school and a jail. Union Steamship boats called twice a week. (The old jail, which doubled as the constable's home, still stands at the corner of Heriot Bay and Green Road, and there are still bars on some of the windows!)

Among the early settlers on the eastern side of the peninsula were Jack Bryant, Tom Baccus and two brothers, Alfred and Walter Joyce. The Joyces had 1,300 acres near Cape Mudge;

Baccus and Bryant chose land near Quathiaski Cove, where Jack built a log cabin in 1888. When the cabin was finished, Jack borrowed a large war canoe from Chief Billy Assu and, in company with Tom, paddled to Comox to pick up his wife Mary and bring her home to Quathiaski. Mary became the first European woman to settle on Quadra. Their daughter Elizabeth, born in 1892, was the first European child born on the island. Arthur Valdes Joyce, born in 1896 to Mr. and Mrs. Alfred Joyce, was the first European boy born on Quadra.

An Indian school opened at Cape Mudge in 1893, at the insistence of R.H. Pidcock. Methodist minister R.J. Walker (sometimes called Johnny) and his wife Agnes were the teachers.

The Twidle store and home at Granite Bay. The store serviced the many settlers there at the turn of the century. Supplies were brought in from Vancouver by Union Steamship. (CRM 7843)

Among the first Finnish settlers in Granite Bay were (left to right) Henry, Heldge, Andy and Emil Luoma. Many Finlanders moved to Granite Bay soon after the turn of the century when the colonization company at Sointula disbanded.

April Point Marina and Yacht Club facilities. During the summer months it is advisable to reserve moorage several months in advance. (Erik Peterson photo)

April Point Lodge is protected by Gowlland Island in Discovery Passage.

Another early settler on that part of the island was Tom Bell, who owned a 191-acre farm between Quathiaski and Gowlland Harbour, surrounded by Pidcock land. In 1894, Bell's land was sold to the Fredrick Yeatman family. Raymond Haas took land next to the missionary Walker near the Cape in 1909.

When Pidcock retired as Indian agent in 1895, he moved his family to the Quathiaski Cove property, where they built a house in traditional English style, with a conservatory, a tennis court and an orchard. The building materials came from a sawmill Pidcock had built. The main room of the house was big enough to serve as a church for the local settlers.

Pidcock, showing a keen sense for business, continued to invest in land. By the turn of the century, he owned all the water frontage in Quathiaski Cove. This included Dick Hall's Trading Post on a wharf at the south end of the cove. When the government replaced the wharf, Pidcock and his sons built a new store on it, as well as a cannery for processing fish. His various business ventures kept his sons fully employed and added to the substantial estate he left on his death in 1902.

Granite Bay, a large, virtually landlocked basin of water on the northwest coast of the island, was also a bustling village near the turn of the century. The first Europeans to settle there were Konstantin Wilhem Stenfors and his family, who moved from Nanaimo in 1903. Alfred Emil Luoma and family moved down from Sointula a couple of years later, when their dreams for a utopia there had come to an end. Other Finnish settlers followed, and soon Granite Bay was known for its large Finnish population.

In 1910, Joseph Dick, the son of Mrs Hosea Bull of Heriot Bay, opened the Granite Bay Hotel. A year later, it was taken over by Henry Twidle, a well-known photographer on the coast. The small hotel did a steady business with the logging industry and offered a shelter from the rain for people waiting for the Union boat.

A public school opened at Granite Bay in 1912. Like many projects on the coast at that time, it was built by community effort: Konstantin Stenfors donated the land, Hastings Mill donated the lumber, men from the mill donated their time and hauled the lumber to the school site by oxen, and Emil Luoma built the school. Miss B.V. Cousins, the first teacher, had twelve students in her one-room school.

From April Point Lodge
and Marina there is a
magnificent view across
Discovery Passage,
where thousands of
seabirds gather to feed
and whales dance a
tango-ballet in the
swiftly running tide.
Cruise ships and other
vessels wait north of here
for slack water in
Seymour Narrows.

Stenfors' daughter Irene married William Stramberg and they lived in Granite Bay for more than forty years, where they were part owners of the Geiler Group of Mines. Stramberg Lake is named in their memory.

Fishing has always been one of the main industries at the south end of Quadra. The cannery built by the Pidcocks in 1904 saw a succession of owners, some of whom were developers and some speculators. In 1906, T.E. Atkins of McDowell–Atkins–Watson took over the cannery. He made some improvements.

then sold it to the Quathiaski Packing Company in 1908. A year later, it was destroyed by fire. The cannery was rebuilt the following year, then transferred to the Quathiaski Canning Company Ltd. W.E. Anderson was the main shareholder of the new company.

Anderson was not only an astute businessman, he was fascinated by the migration of the salmon. He noticed that the sockeye running past the cannery were different, depending on what river they appeared to be heading for when they were caught. He turned this information over to the Fisheries Department, which confirmed his observations. Further studies based on this data resulted in our present knowledge of the life cycle of salmonid fishes.

The Anderson cannery, like many along the

Below left: I caught two
good-sized cohoe while
fishing with a guide from
April Point.

Below right: When the
April Point Lodge first
opened, guests, luggage
and freight were ferried
across Discovery Passage
by landing barge from
the Spit at Painter's
Lodge.

Seen from April Point, a seiner heads north through Discovery Passage.

Launching a tyee boat at April Point marina. The outboard engine is used only to travel to and from the fishing grounds. Only rowing is permitted when fishing under Tyee Club rules.

coast at that time, especially those dealing with native Indians, issued metal tokens instead of cash as a payment for fish. The tokens came in three sizes, varied in value from one to one hundred fish, and could be traded for goods only in the cannery store. It was far cheaper to buy groceries and other supplies in Vancouver and have them shipped in by steamship than to purchase them in cannery stores. Chief Billy Assu was largely responsible for having the system changed so that fishermen received cash.

In 1938, British Columbia Packers, which was buying most of the smaller canneries on the coast, took over the Anderson cannery at Quathiaski. It was destroyed by fire three years later and was not rebuilt.

The first motorized water taxis operating between Quathiaski Cove and Campbell River went into service in 1914. One of the early taxi operators was Harry Poole, who had a sixteen-foot clinker-built rowboat with a 3½ horse-power engine. Another was Harry Sykes, who had a thirty-five-foot cabin cruiser.

Even when Phil and Phyllis Peterson first came to Campbell River in the 1940s, the water taxi service was primitive. This did not discourage them, however, from moving eventually to the Gowlland Harbour side of the Passage. When they first came to Campbell River, they booked into Painters Lodge. Phil, a former publishing executive from California, had come to fish for tyee salmon and relax in the wilderness setting. The spectacular scenery and way of life so impressed the couple that on a subsequent visit they bought land at April Point, across the channel from the R.H. Pidcock estate.

At that time there were six old bachelors living in shacks and eking out a living at April Point. Because of the men's hardships, the area had come to be known as "Poverty Point." But to its residents, Poverty Point was a haven of refuge. Their backyards were filled with flowers and vegetables. At their doorstep was a quiet cove where their rowboats lay secured to log floats protected from storms. Beyond the harbour and rocky headlands of April Point was a splendid view of the Inside Passage, where thousands of seabirds gathered to feed and killer whales in transit danced a tango with the swift running tide. The old gents never had a feeling of loneliness as boats heading through Seymour Narrows often stopped in the small harbour to wait for slack tide. One of the men, Jim Brant, loved animals, and fostered a young seal pup, which came to a rock in front of his shack each day for a meal of herring.

When the Petersons purchased April Point, they invited the old-timers to continue living there, but the men decided they would have to find another place to live. The Petersons understood. To help them get re-established, they paid them for the cookstoves that were too heavy to move by rowboat. Early one morning, the men dipped their oars into the quiet waters of Gowlland Harbour and left April Point behind forever. In the wake of Jim Brant's boat swam his pet seal, obviously determined to join his master in his new home.

The year April Point was purchased, Phil Peterson took a sabbatical from his publishing business. He intended to spend the time relaxing and building a place where the family could spend their summer vacation. Neither he nor Phyllis had planned on starting a resort. However, their plans changed overnight when some visitors arrived in Quathiaski Cove without a place to stay. The Petersons offered them one of the shacks that the "old gents" had vacated. That happened in 1945, and it was the beginning of the April Point Resort.

As the resort developed, Phil Peterson extended his one-year sabbatical to two. Eventually, he quit the publishing business and

moved his family to April Point. Their three youngest children, June, Erik and Thor, were in public school when they moved. Their eldest son, Warren, was in the US Navy. The children loved living at April Point, in spite of the fact that they had to walk through underbrush on a makeshift trail to school. That trail has become the road from Quathiaski Cove to April Point.

April Point, like Painters Lodge in Campbell River, was a family project. "We all helped out with the chores," said Thor. "After school there was never much time to play, instead we came home and helped carry the rocks to build the swimming pool, lumber for the buildings or any other chores that had to be done. If some of our buddies came home with us from school, they had to work as well!" When Warren came home on a furlough, he spent thirty-seven of his forty days off working on the swimming pool. With the cannery at Quathiaski closed, the Petersons built their own cannery at April Point in the late 1940s. It is still in operation, now owned by Walcan.

To help transport freight, passengers and building supplies from Campbell River, the Petersons bought a used landing craft they named *David Lee*. Guests left their cars at the spit near Painters Lodge and boarded the *David Lee* for the trip across Discovery Passage.

From the row of shacks along the beach, April Point has developed into a world-class resort, stretching along three miles of shore-

line and including more than 200 acres of forested land. There is a rustic lodge built on the rocky headland and cottages with hot tubs and fireplaces tucked among the trees, commanding a sweeping view of Discovery Passage. Farther along the waterfront, there is a public marina with 5,000 feet of moorage, as well as power, water, a laundromat, a store and marine repair facilities.

Some things at April Point are much the same as they were in the 1940s, like the big swimming pool in front of the lodge, and the Peterson family itself. Although Phil Peterson died more than a decade ago, Phyllis, who celebrated her eighty-second birthday in the summer of 1991, and Warren and Erik have remained as authentic and as charming as their surroundings. They still give as much love and care to their guests in their wilderness paradise as they did more than forty years ago.

South Quadra settlers' houses and cabins on the shore of Discovery Passage.

Left: Warren (at left) and Erik Peterson and their mother, Phyllis. They are the founders, builders and longtime hosts of April Point Lodge.

Below: Looking north toward Seymour Narrows from the April Point marina.

7. Heriot Bay

Heriot Bay, on the grassy shores of southern Quadra Island, attracted settlers from around the world more than a hundred years ago. Situated near the junction of Sutil and Hoskyn channels, the land faces the spectacular mountain formations of the Coast Range, sometimes snow-capped and shrouded with mist. It is said to be the home of the spirit that watches over Desolation Sound.

The Salish Indians were the first inhabitants of the land around Heriot Bay, and they were eventually driven out by the more aggressive Kwakiutl people. Evidence of the battles fought between the two nations is still visible on Rebecca Spit, where in the shade of the tall Douglas fir, open grassy fields are partially surrounded by a semi-circular trench and embankment. Archaeologists believe they were fortifications built by the Salish Indians while trying to defend themselves against the Kwakiutl between the sixteenth and eighteenth centuries. By the time Europeans came to settle, Quadra belonged to the Kwakiutl.

Logging was the main industry on southern Quadra Island during the first part of this century, but the area also attracted fishermen, trappers and a few miners who had built their shacks in the many small bays. Local people knew Heriot Bay simply as "the Bay," where they picked up their mail and got supplies. The Bay was the supply and trading centre for Desolation Sound at the turn of the century, and it still is today.

Hosea Bull was the most important of the early settlers in Heriot Bay. He arrived on southern Quadra in the early 1890s. He had an eye to the future and, soon after arriving, bought most of the foreshore land around the bay. Then he and his partner, Charles Hodak, cleared the land and built the first Heriot Bay Hotel and saloon, complete with a brass rail around the bar and spittoons for the tobacco chewers and smokers. The hotel and saloon officially opened in the summer of 1894. Business was slow at first, but by bushwhacking a trail through eight miles of dense underbrush to Gowlland Harbour on the other side of the island, the partners created easy access for travellers from Discovery Passage. After that, the hotel had a full house every weekend.

With the hotel doing a booming business, Bull and Hodak went ahead and built a store and post office. Bull was the sparkplug of the partnership. He was soon operating a logging camp and sawmill to supply the lumber for his own projects and for other construction in the

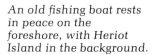

An old fishing boat rests in peace on the foreshore, with Heriot Island in the background.

area. As well, he continued his original trade as a baker, supplying fresh bread to nearby logging camps, ships and inhabitants of the growing village.

Helen, Hosea Bull's second wife, was a New Zealander, refined and good-looking with prematurely snow-white hair and a snow-white Pomeranian dog that followed her everywhere. It was Helen's ambition to change her husband's rough and rowdy drinking establishment into a dining and vacation resort catering to the elite strata of society, whose members travelled the coast in their private yachts or aboard Union Steamship boats. She set her mind to getting rid of customers like Tom Leask, a small, soft-spoken man with the distressing habit of biting chunks out of his beer glasses and lining the pieces up along the saloon bar. He was giving the hotel the kind of publicity that Helen didn't want.

Helen must have seemed a heaven-sent gift to the missionaries working the coast at the time. She helped create an atmosphere in the hotel where proper Sunday services could be conducted. Until Helen arrived, the missionaries had been attempting to deliver their sermons in the saloon. Often their oratory was interrupted by the rolling of the dice and the cries of the card players. One missionary was

so dedicated that he took orders for liquor and cards, then made his purchases at Shoal Bay, the vice centre of the coast where drinking, gambling and prostitution were wide open. Then, before turning the goods over to the men, he would go to their homes to give them lectures on the evils of drinking and gambling.

But the practice of these vices around Heriot Bay came to a temporary halt in the spring of 1912, when the hotel burned to the ground. There was no fire-fighting equipment, so once the flames took hold the entire structure was destroyed, with the exception of the stone chimney—which is still in use in the present Heriot Bay Inn. Having the old hotel wiped out by fire must have seemed a blessing to Helen Bull. Now she and Hosea could build the kind of place she wanted. The new hotel was built in a grand style. There was still a saloon offering refreshment to weary fishermen and loggers, but more genteel folk were served in a number of elegant rooms. There were nineteen bedrooms and a dance hall on the second floor, as well as a large verandah on the main floor, with hanging baskets of flowers, where summer dances took place. There was also an aviary with lush foliage where rare songbirds were kept, as well as a

Aerial view of Heriot Bay and Heriot Island, with Rebecca Spit in the background. (George McNutt photo)

pool behind the hotel where the owners' pet seal lived. Crystal and china were used in the dining room and the hotel staff were dressed in white uniforms.

People who came to Heriot Bay to book passage on a Union steamship often waited several hours before the vessel arrived. Helen Bull, a warm and hospitable woman in spite of her aversion to rowdy behaviour, invited them to spend the time at the hotel.

One of the most lavish functions held at the time was the christening of a new steam launch used to transport visitors at the hotel to nearby places of interest. When the day arrived, some 300 guests gathered at the hotel. Long banquet tables covered in white linen and silver and crystal place settings stood on the lawn beneath the huge maple trees. Exquisite cut flowers and silk flags were placed at each setting. On the upper deck of the launch stood Hosea's son, eight-year-old Cecil Bull, clothed in white duck, inviting all the guests who could find standing room on the launch to come aboard.

Following the champagne christening of the vessel by Mrs Bull, three women in sheer white flowing gowns stood on the bow of the vessel and recited a poem composed for the occasion.

This incarnation of the Heriot Bay Hotel was a great success under the management of Helen Bull, but eventually it too was destroyed by fire. It was later rebuilt and had a number of owners over the years. In the early 1980s, Lyle Acton and Angela Plasterer took

over, renaming it the Heriot Bay Inn. They worked twenty-four hours a day trying to get the place back in shape. The pub was the only part of the hotel that had remained open through the years, and the only guest seemed to be a ghost that occasionally slept in one of the rooms. "We never saw anyone, and whoever it was never paid their bill," said Lyle. The inn has been restored and the rooms tastefully renovated in Victorian style. The moderate prices include a heritage bed and breakfast in a family-style restaurant, with indoor or outdoor dining. The ghost has disappeared.

By the turn of the century, Heriot Bay had become an established village with a hotel, school, post office and mission. As well, it was a scheduled stop for the Union Steamship Company. Captain Ian Morrison, one of the skippers of that grand fleet of ships, reminisced with me one afternoon about the early days on the coast. "One of the most difficult places to bring a ship into was Heriot Bay," he said. "In the winter it was usually dark and likely there'd be a stiff northeaster on our stern. The real challenge of course was reversing out of the bay, and with the wind coming from that direction it's somewhat of miracle we never hit those rocks!" Now in his eighties, Captain Morrison's eyes hold the reflection of the sea, and his lined face contains the wisdom that comes from having lived afloat. He has been retired for a number of years and is the sole surviver of those legendary captains of the ships with the black funnels.

The first telephone service to southern

Quadra came in 1910. The submerged cable ran from the mainland via Cortes and Marina islands to Quathiaski Cove and then to Grouse Island. From there, it continued overland across the island and then followed the ocean floor to Campbell River. The Quathiaski Cove terminus was called Bagot Station, after Trevor Bagot, the first lineman.

The telephone cable at the bottom of Discovery Passage was a hazard to ships anchored there while awaiting slack tide in Seymour Narrows. One angry captain, his anchor snarled in the cable, threatened to cut it free. When the lineman told him it would cost him $5 a foot to replace, he cut his anchor line instead and continued north with the tide.

Mining, logging and fishing were the main industries on Quadra Island. The best-known mine was the Lucky Jim, located between Stranberg Lake and Granite Bay. Lucky Jim was owned by Great Granite Development Syndicate, in which Eric Hamber, a former BC lieutenant governor, was a shareholder. The famous locomotive Curly hauled 1,200 tons of gold and copper a month out of the Lucky Jim mine.

Curly, a saddle-type number three locomotive, was manufactured in 1869 by Marshuetts and Cantrell of San Francisco for a contractor building the sea wall there. It was used in the building of the Panama Canal, then shipped to BC, where it was used in the construction of the Canadian Pacific Railway in 1881. When the CPR contract ended, Curly was sold to the Hastings Sawmill Company, which put it to work in Mud Bay near White Rock, then Rock Bay on Vancouver Island. Curly ended up in Granite Bay on Quadra Island, where it was used in both logging and mining. Curly is believed to have been the first logging locomotive in British Columbia. It retired in 1926 and now resides at Heritage Village in Burnaby.

In 1925, during a long, hot summer, a great forest fire fanned by a fresh northwest wind swept over Quadra's tinder-dry land, destroying everything in its path. Countless animals, birds and other forest creatures were caught in the inferno. Many people were left homeless, lucky to escape with their lives. The fire, which began at the Hastings logging operation in Granite Bay and burned almost to Cape Mudge before dying out, was the worst the island has ever known.

In Heriot Bay the late Francis Dickie, a well-known writer, and his wife Suzanne were among the lucky ones who escaped. They saw the fire coming and began packing their most valued possessions, then carried them down to their rowboat on the beach. When the boat would hold no more, they took stock of what they had on board. Their cargo included an armful of books (out of a library of 2,000), a galvanized bathtub full of household treasures, two Airedale dogs and three cats. Fortu-

Gilbert Krook, sitting on a fish scow belonging to the Canadian Fishing Company.

nately, in the nick of time, the Columbia Mission ship *Rendezvous* arrived towing a raft with two fire pumps, and the Dickies' house was saved.

In spite of disasters, Heriot Bay has survived as a village. Many of the people who pioneered the coast, or their children, still live there. Jerry and Susan Enns and Susan's brother, Norman Dowler, are now the principal owners of the Heriot Bay store, which Norman and Susan's parents owned before them. Norman was four years old when the family arrived in Heriot Bay, where he grew up and went to school. He worked on the tugs before getting into the retail business. The store is located near the head of the government wharf where Hosea Bull's sawmill once stood. It is twice the size of the original one, which was destroyed by fire in 1978, and it includes a post office and a liquor store.

Gilbert and Muriel Krook are two more long-time residents. Muriel, the second youngest of the Chapman girls from Big Bay on Stuart Island, met Gilbert and married him when he was fishing at Stuart Island. Gilbert, who was born at St. Paul's Hospital in Vancouver, has lived most of his life on the coast. He remembers living in a tent behind Hansens' log house in Port Neville. "I had to have goat's milk, and we kept a goat in a shed near the tent. One night while we were over at the Hansens', a cougar gnawed through the door and then killed our goat. That was terrible!" The Krook family moved from Port Neville to Quathiaski Cove in the early 1920s and settled near the old ferry landing. In 1927, they towed their house around Cape Mudge to Heriot Bay. With the help of Roy Yeatman and his old truck, they hauled it up on the beach and, eventually, some distance up the road where it

The rebuilt Heriot Bay Inn as it looks today. A fishing boat is moored at the inn's docking area.

stands today, a small white house surrounded by fruit trees and flowers.

"There was always music around the house when I grew up, everyone played something. When I was fifteen, Dad bought me an accordion and then sent me to Vancouver to take lessons from Alf Carlson. Alf used to log on Quadra and lived with my parents in 1924–25. I could read music, but could play very little when I went to Alf. It was unbelievable after two weeks practising four to five hours a day I came home playing the accordion. He was a great teacher!"

Gilbert was one of four musicians who made up the Rhythm Busters, one of the most popular "touring bands," groups that travelled the coast playing at Saturday night dances. The other three musicians were his father, Ture Krook, who played the zither, his brother Elmer, who played the drums, and his uncle Lars, who played the violin.

In 1960, Gilbert went to work as first mate and relieving skipper on the BC ferry that shuttles between Quathiaski Cove and Campbell River. To his surprise, the captain of the ferry was an old friend, Tom Hall. They had gone through grade school together and written their high school entrance exams at the same time in Campbell River. From that time they had gone different ways and had not seen each other for twenty-five years. Gilbert is retired now and lives in Heriot Bay.

There have been changes around Heriot Bay since the turn of the century. One that is certainly for the better is in the education system. The first public school, which opened in 1894, was for white children only. Today's school is much bigger and is open to children of every colour and creed. Other things have remained the same, like the ancient plum and apple trees that shade the "Esplanade." They were planted and given to the community, along with the walkway along the shore, by Hosea Bull back near the turn of the century.

Today the marina has 1,200 feet of moorage, with diesel, gas, propane and outboard fuel on the dock. For boaters, Heriot Bay is only a short distance from most of the favourite places on this part of the coast. The anchorage in Drew Harbour on the western side of the spit is well protected. Boats can be left there in safety while the owners enjoy a swim and a picnic on the beach or in the open meadows where fierce battles were once fought between Indian tribes. Rebecca Spit is now a provincial marine park. Like the rest of Desolation Sound, the water surrounding the spit is warmer than other parts of the coast during the summer months.

There are many good walking trails around Heriot Bay. One can take a bike or car along the short distance to the other side of the island, have lunch at the April Point Lodge, or visit the famous Kwagiulth Museum at Quathiaski. One favourite trip of mine is to head down to Cape Mudge. When I look south over the Strait of Georgia from the 200-foot cliff, I imagine I am Lieutenant Mayne who in 1860, at that viewpoint, noted in his diary: "This part of the Gulf of Georgia forms a playground for waters, in which they frolic, utterly regardless of all tidal rules!"

8. Cortes Island and its Villages

Cortes Island lies at the heart of the cruising area of Desolation Sound. It measures about twenty miles in length from north to south, and about ten miles in width. The shape of the island roughly resembles an octopus. Its winding arms have provided sheltered harbours for Salish canoes in centuries past, and for the modern yachts of today.

In the early summer of 1792, the British exploring vessels *Chatham* and *Discovery*, under the command of Captain George Vancouver, and the Spanish ships *Mexicana* and *Sutil*, under commander Cayetano Valdes, explored and charted the coast and waters surrounding the "octopus." The ships often shared the same anchorages, and the officers became friends. Cortes, Hernando and Marina islands, Cortes Bay and Sutil Channel are all named in memory of the Spanish explorers.

The Salish Indians navigated the channels around Cortes long before the coming of the Europeans. They fought bitter wars against the enemy Kwakiutl people, who were advancing southward down the coast. Gorge Harbour on the southwest shore of the island was one of the last strongholds of the Salish people. It is said they rolled large boulders down the steep cliffs onto the enemy canoes trying to attack through the narrow channel. The Salish must have been victorious at least this once, as the battle is celebrated in pictographs painted on the cliffs at the entrance to this almost land-locked basin of water.

Whaletown, a small protected harbour a few miles north of the Gorge, was the site of the first European development on Cortes. It took its name from the Dawson and Douglass Whaling Company, which based its operations here between 1869 and 1870. The forty-seven-ton schooner *Kate* was used to chase down and harpoon the whales. They were then hauled ashore, where their livers and blubber were removed and the rest of the carcasses were left on the beach to rot. It must have been a gruesome and noisome spectacle.

Whales were plentiful in the Strait of Georgia when Dawson and other companies began harvesting them. However, there was no closed season on the big mammals. Pregnant females and mothers with calves were shown no mercy; the calves could be heard screaming as their mothers were slaughtered. The Dawson company extracted over 20,000 gallons of whale oil during their two years on Cortes Island. By the summer of 1871, the *British Colonist* newspaper noted that whales were scarce in the Strait. The Dawson Whaling Company, which had moved its base to Hornby Island, was already in receivership.

For the next fifteen years, Cortes Island remained in its primeval state of wilderness, visited only by an occasional lonely hand-logger

The narrow channel into Gorge Harbour. From the tall cliffs, natives defended the entrance by hurling boulders at intruders. Pictographs can be seen on the left, a few feet above high water.

Whaletown wharf on Cortes Island, looking north. The bay opposite, where small white buildings can be seen, is the approximate location of the old whaling station.

or prospector rowing the coast in search of a fortune. Then, in 1886, Michael Manson, a native of the Shetland Islands, and his partner, George Leask, travelled together from Comox in their small sailing sloop to become the first Europeans to settle on the island.

Michael Manson was joined on Cortes by his brother, John, in 1888. During the first few years the brothers lived on the island, they acquired considerable property, including Mitlenatch and Hernando islands. Unlike many of the developers who were taking over coastal land near the turn of the century, the Mansons were conservationists. Conscious of the environment, they took a conservative approach to development that helped maintain the pristine beauty of Desolation Sound. Manson's Landing is named in memory of these distinguished pioneers.

In 1893, a government survey of Cortes was completed and the land on the island was opened for pre-emption. This meant that if a settler lived on the land six months a year for

ten years and cleared the trees and brush from ten acres, it belonged to him.

Names of settlers living on Cortes near the turn of the century included Tiber, Coulter (of Coulter Bay), Corby, Miles, Percival, Shufer, Thompson, Vincent, Burridge, Trahey, Halcrow, Rose, Heay, Vaughan, Seaton and McNeel. In 1885, the community opened a school at Gunflint Lake in a log cabin on the Horace Heay property.

One of the early visitors to the island was Alice-Mary Allen, who was a missionary in India like her father before her. In the early 1890s, Alice-Mary travelled twice from Delhi to Cortes Island by ship to visit her brothers, Wilf, Jim and Charles, who had settled at Gorge Harbour after attending private school in Seattle. On her last furlough, she told them that if she ever married and had children, she would like to live on Cortes Island. On her return to Delhi, she met her husband, David Robertson, a Scottish soldier who was stationed in India. Two years later, after his discharge from the army, they were married.

In 1898, the young couple embarked for Vancouver. Instead of sailing from India across the Pacific, Alice-Mary, her husband and their new baby, Allen, took passage on the schooner *Esmeralda*, bound south around Cape Horn. Mary-Alice loved the ocean, and whenever the weather was fair she was out on deck with Allen in her arms, watching the ever-changing sea. Unfortunately, the long ocean passage played havoc with David's health. Unlike his wife, he was prone to seasickness, and by the time they reached Vancouver he was dehydrated and had lost a lot of weight. He never did regain his health.

Like many immigrants to Canada at that time, the Robertsons had meagre savings. They had barely enough to purchase a lot near 10th and Cambie, where Vancouver City Hall is today. Their nearest neighbour was a mile

The steam catcher boat Orion, belonging to the Pacific Whaling Company, chasing a whale off Vancouver Island. (BCARS 65295)

A community picnic on the sand beach at Hague Lake, Cortes Island, about 1919.

away, along a dirt road winding through trees and brush. They had to clear their own lot before building a place to live. David had apprenticed as a carpenter in his youth and in spite of his ailing condition managed to build a cozy little cabin for them.

In general, life was easier than they had expected. David, gifted in working with wood, found steady employment at the Stamp Mill in Gastown, and Alice-Mary worked the land. They had two more children, Meg and Rankin. Then disaster struck the family. David, whose health had stabilized somewhat, contracted rheumatoid arthritis. He became bedridden and unable to work. Their money soon ran out, and Alice-Mary decided to move the family to Cortes Island where her brothers were living.

I spent a wonderful afternoon talking to Meg (Robertson) Shaw in her comfortable home near the beach in Whaletown. Then in

her eighties, Meg reminisced about coming to live on Cortes Island. Her father was very ill and in continuous pain, but her mother never complained and, with the help of Allen, her oldest brother, cleared the land and built a house. Besides looking after her own family, Alice-Mary worked as a practical nurse, caring for the sick and delivering babies. She was the

Mrs. Louisa Tooker on the porch of her cedar-log home, Coulter Bay, Cortes Island, with dog Buddie. Mrs. Tooker was a well-known member of the community; the present Whaletown library is named after her.

David Morrison driving a team at John Manson's horse-logging show, about 1918.

Spring flowers bloom on rocky outcrops around Whaletown store, Cortes Island.

An old logging pulley in Whaletown.

A view of Whaletown from the home of Bill Emery, a Whaletown resident.

only trained medical person on Cortes Island at the time. Duncan, her youngest child, was born while the family was living on Cortes.

When the Robertson family arrived in Whaletown in 1905, there were six families living there. Amenities included a school, a store–trading post–saloon, a post office, a wharf and the services of the Union Steamship Company. Miss Bland was the schoolteacher and Mr. Drinkwater was the merchant. The little village was isolated from the rest of the island. There were no connecting roads to the other villages, and the only way to Gorge Harbour or Manson's Landing was by boat. In 1910, a submerged telephone cable was laid between Cortes and Sara Point on the mainland. It continued across to Quathiaski Cove on Quadra Island and from there to Campbell River.

Dances were the main social event, as in most other villages on the coast. Almost every Saturday night there would be a dance somewhere, and people would come from far and near to attend. Elmer Elingson from Cortes Island or the Rhythm Busters from Heriot Bay usually supplied the music. There were a lot of Scandinavians working around the coast at that time in both logging and fishing. Some of them ran their own stills. They were a lively bunch, and at some time during the evening one of the Norwegians would invariably leap on a bench and shout the time-honoured battle cry: "Ten thousand Swedes ran through the weeds, chased by one Norwegian!" Sometimes the Swedes took exception and the evening ended in a glorious free-for-all.

Until the 1930s, Squirrel Cove was classified as an Indian reserve and Manson's Landing and Whaletown were the active centres on Cortes. Both had stores and post offices

Squirrel Cove has a government dock, store and post office. The Indian reserve can be seen on the opposite shore.

Refuge Cove on Redonda Island is an important fuelling and supply centre.

The Robertson family of Cortes Island. Seated: parents Mr. and Mrs. D. Robertson. Standing (left to right): Rankin Robertson, Gwyneth Robertson, Meg (Robertson) Shaw, Alan Robertson, Alice Shaw, Dorothy (Mrs. A.) Robertson, Winifred Robertson and Duncan Robertson.

The Whaletown trading post during the winter of 1949–50. The building houses the present store.

and the Union steamship stopped at each point at least once a week. Jim Allen had a small store in Gorge Harbour, but it was mainly for staple goods. Other harbours around the island were virtually isolated.

Through the years, the main industries on the island were logging and fishing. Almost every homesteader engaged in one or the other of these occupations, and some supplemented their income by selling produce to the logging camps.

When the Fraser River Sawmill Company was operating in Coulter Bay in the early part of the century, the timber business on the island was carried out on a big scale with deepsea vessels coming in to pick up lumber. When the island was logged off, however, the company moved, and many settlers also relocated.

With many people leaving Cortes, some of the people who remained approached the Union Steamship Company with the idea of starting special excursions to the island. Once visitors had seen its beauty, it was hoped, they would surely be tempted to settle there! The company liked the idea and began to offer a weekend cruise to Savary and Cortes islands, as well as Toba Inlet, a 360-mile round trip—including meals—for only $12. Many people took advantage of the inexpensive cruise, but because of the lack of industry, few came back to settle on Cortes.

The Union steamships were a vital link for the villagers. If for some reason one of the ships was out of service, it caused considerable anxiety. The Union steamships brought in supplies for villagers, most of whom had accounts with J.P. Spencer and Woodward's in Vancouver. When I was a child living on the coast, I can remember my mother making out the shopping list. She gave it to one of us kids, who rowed it over to the steamship landing to make sure it got in the mail. The following week, we met the ship and anxiously waited for our supplies. The people working for Woodward's and Spencer's seldom missed sending everything in the order.

The Columbia Coast Mission was another vital link for these small communities. The mission looked after the needy by bringing in clothing, medical supplies or a doctor, and sometimes a dentist, to those who would otherwise have done without. Alan Greene, well-known for his missionary work along the coast, had his headquarters at Whaletown in the early part of the century. Travelling aboard a fourteen-foot open gasboat, he visited a congregation that stretched from Desolation Sound to Kelsey Bay.

Between the early 1930s and the late 1960s, lifestyles around Cortes remained much the same. Then, in 1967, the road connecting the south and north ends of the island was completed. Two years later, the ferry *Cortes Queen* swung into service between Heriot Bay and Whaletown. In 1970, electricity came to the island.

Today Cortes has about 700 full-time residents. As on many of the coastal islands in BC, a number of writers, painters and sculptors have taken up full-time residence there. Besides arts and crafts, there are "retreats" like Hollyhock Farms on the southern peninsula, offering specialized workshops that attract people from all over the world.

There are a number of tourist facilities on the island, including Cortes Bay Marine Resort, Gorge Harbour Marine Resort and Gorge View Marina, with excellent facilities for boaters and campers. As well there are good hiking trails and swimming at Cortes Bay. At Squirrel Cove, you will find a government float that has limited moorage, with fuel and water available. There is also a store, a liquor store and a post office. At Whaletown, the terminus for the Quadra Island ferry, there are a store, a post office, a library up the road and limited moorage at a government docks. Mansons Landing Marine Park has a government dock with temporary moorage only, and some facilities for boaters and other visitors. The park was established in 1973 to protect the wonderful sand beaches.

Located at the heart of Desolation Sound, Cortes is an ideal headquarters for boaters,

Above: Violet Anderson's school class at Squirrel Cove, Cortes Island, 1941.

Left: The view south from Whaletown, with Marina Island in the background.

Below: The Milstead homestead on Cortes Island. Al and Pierrette Milstead spent many years carrying supplies from island to island in their old tugboat.

Below: A menu from the Union Steamship vessel Camosun *details the gargantuan holiday feast for New Year's diners in 1957. The menu credits the Master, Chief Engineer and Purser, but not, curiously, the chef. The menu's back cover (right) shows the Union Steamship routes up the coast from Victoria to Alaska.*

with numerous protected anchorages, excellent facilities and spectacular scenery—and a long history as a centre of coastal activity. A prediction made by Lukin Johnston in 1925 in the Sunday *Province* has finally come true: "Some day Cortes Island will be discovered by tired Vancouver and Victoria businessmen. Every bay on this 15 mile long island presents a vista of beauty, where one feels the desire to erect a summer home. There are lovely prospects of sea and foliage at every turn. An ideal peaceful place to forget the cars and noise of the city!"

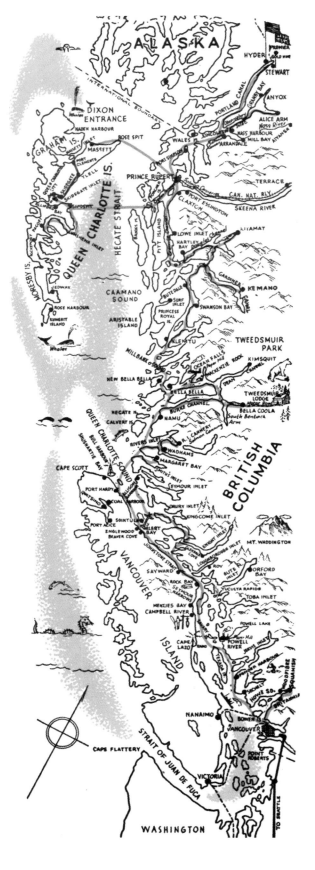

S.S. "Camosun"

On Board
W.McCombe
Master

Jan.1st,1957.
Date

F.Smith
Chief Engineer
R.Stover
Purser
N.Davidson
Chief Steward

NEW YEARS DINNER

Celery en Branche   Queen Olives
Fresh Shrimpmeat Cocktail

·

Cream of Oyster Soup

·

Poached Spring Salmon,Parsley Sauce

·

Chicken Salad,Mayonnaise

·

Baked York Ham,Sweet Potatoes
Fresh Crabmeat,ala Newburg

·

Roast Prime Ribs of Beef,Yorkshire Pudding
Roast Stuffed Tom Turkey,Cranberry Sauce

·

Steamed or Mashed Potatoes
Brussel Sprouts

·

Steamed English Plum Pudding,Hard Sauce
Hot or Cold Mince Pie
Apple Pie   Xmas Cake
Strawberry Jello,Whipped Cream
Vanilla Ice Cream

·

Canadian,Kraft or McLarens Cheese
·
Fresh Fruit   Scotch Mints
Tea   Milk   Buttermilk   Coffee

 Union Steamships wish all patrons
A Merry Christmas
A Happy New Year

9. Owen Bay

Owen Bay, on the southeastern shore of Sonora Island, near the junction of the Hole In The Wall with the Okisollo Rapids, lies about 120 miles north of Vancouver by boat. It is a serene, almost landlocked harbour that casts an eerie spell. On a full running tide, the roar of the rapids can be heard in the distance.

The pass leading into Owen Bay has a rock to the left marked by kelp. We used to jig for cod there when we were kids. To the right there are several small islets between the pass and Springer Point on the main shore of Sonora Island.

Sonora Island was named in 1903 in memory of the Spanish schooner *Sonora* commanded by Juan Francisco de la Bodega Quadra, the Spanish naval officer who explored and charted the British Columbia coast in 1791. Owen Bay was named by Captain David Pender, R.N., master of the surveying vessel *Beaver* in 1864, after Commander Fredrick John Owen Evans, R.N., of the Admiralty Hydrogaphic Office.

In Owen Bay there are many smaller bays and coves, sheltered by rocky bluffs covered with sweet-smelling pine trees and golden moss. On the northeastern side, there is a high cliff. A great gash has been taken out of its sheer face, as if from the shock of some heavy object. When we lived in Owen Bay in the 1930s and as youngsters, we were told a meteorite had landed there many years ago. Looking for fragments of the meteorite was one of our favourite summer excursions, though we had no idea what to look for as we searched among the rubble at the bottom of the cliff.

I thought about Owen Bay many years later while I was sailing across the Indian Ocean aboard the *Kelea*. It was about two o'clock in the morning, I was on watch when suddenly I felt a glow of heat and the ocean around me lit up as bright as day, as a deafening crackling-hissing sound came from above. It was an experience I will never forget. I sat frozen in the cockpit for many minutes wondering if it might happen again. Watching the stars twinkling in the sky, I realized that a meteorite had come down into the ocean—like the one that hit the cliff in Owen Bay.

Owen Bay was first occupied in the early 1900s by loggers working for the Pacific Coast and Chemainus Lumber Company, with timber leases there and at Venture Point. When the company moved its operations elsewhere,

the workmen moved as well. The exception was Harry Pedersen, known as "Whisky Harry" because he liked an occasional drink. Harry stayed on and worked the land at Owen Bay. His homestead occupied the foreshore and the land directly behind what remains of the government dock today. For a long time the bay belonged to Harry. There was always a cup of coffee and a chew of snuff or some vegetables from the garden for folks who dropped by. Some visitors, like August Schnarr and Logan Schibler, stayed on and settled. No one knows what happened to Harry; one day he just dis-

The Logan and Gunhilde Schibler house, Owen Bay, 1950. The Schiblers were early settlers in Owen Bay.

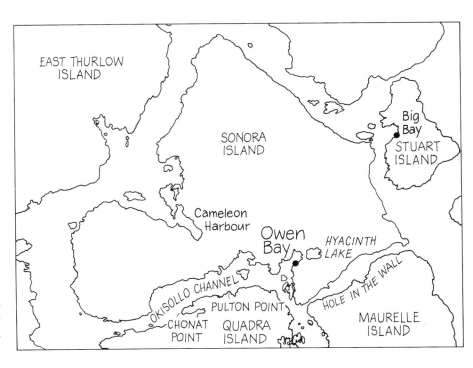

Aerial view of Owen Bay log booming area and Hyacinth Lake. (George McNutt photo)

appeared. Some people said he drowned. His body was never found.

The Schibler family moved to Owen Bay in 1925 and built a good-sized house on Harry's property. They later became the centre of the growing community. August Schnarr came all the way to Owen Bay from Oregon in a rowboat. He was a rugged man who earned an income logging, trapping, fishing and hunting cougars for bounty. One of his traplines lay along a trail that connected Owen Bay to Cameleon Harbour on the northwest side of Sonora Island, where the Lansell family had a

Helen, Jack and Jean Schibler, Raza Island, 1924.

homestead. Schnarr married one of the beautiful Lansell daughters and the newlyweds settled in Owen Bay on the property that once belonged to Harry.

In the late 1920s, Schnarr was well known along the coast as a cougar hunter. He used dogs to corner or tree the big cats before shooting them. Once, in Owen Bay, in the forest directly behind our floathouse, he shot a milk-laden female cougar. Later, hunting around in the bush, he found four cubs, their eyes still closed, crying for their mother. He threw the cubs in his pack and carried them home, for the sake of the bounty on each head. Mrs. Schnarr was dead by this time, and the three daughters persuaded him to spare the orphaned cubs. They fed them canned milk from a coke bottle with a nipple on the end, and managed to save two males and one female. They named the cubs Cleo, Leo and Gilmore.

Somehow the cubs must have known that it was a man that had killed their mother, because they purred like kittens when women came to see them, but growled or hissed if a man came too close. When they were young, they were allowed to romp around the house, but when they grew older they were kept outside and chained to prevent them from going after the neighbours' chickens or other small animals. Gilmore lived for only a few months, but Leo lived for two years and Cleo lived for six.

A number of other people settled in Owen

Bay in the 1920s, including Justine Door, Billy Walters and Harry Shoot. There were also transients who stayed for a few days or months living in their rowboats, pitching tents, or building ramshackle lean-tos. Money was scarce and it was a meagre existence that the land provided in the Dirty Thirties. Yet there was a community spirit and by the end of the decade there were half a dozen families living in Owen Bay. The majority had children, and the one-room school boasted a class of twelve.

Aside from the Schiblers, the three main homesteads in the bay belonged to the Extines, the Walters and the Vanderests. The latter two had land near the head of the bay. The Extines' property was on the northwestern side near the "Pass" where there is now only a grassy field and a few wild roses clinging to old timbers. My main memory of Mrs. Extine is that she always had peanut butter cookies for the children.

My family, the Hansens, had a floathouse in the small cove across the bay from the Extine homestead. Our floating camp had been towed down from Loughborough Inlet, were my father had worked for the Hastings Logging Company. We lived in Owen Bay for a couple of years and then moved across the Okisollo Channel to a homestead on Quadra Island that stretched along the waterfront between Pulton and Chonat Bay points.

Our homestead on Quadra had a good stand of timber and my father and his partner, Ole Olsen, horse-logged there for a number of years. I can remember going to where they were logging with a lunch pail for my dad, walking along the old skid road, listening to the trees talking to me as the wind blew through the branches, and the horses neighing to me as they saw me coming down the road. They are good memories.

Between 1925 and 1960, the Schibler home was the heart of Owen Bay. Other families came and went but there was always one

member of the Schibler family living there. They were the unelected mayors who would see that there were enough children in the bay to keep the school open, organize social events, and on many occasions bring in the mail and groceries from nearby Waiatt Bay or Surge Narrows.

People with children were encouraged to settle in the Bay. At one point there were as many as twenty students enrolled in the school. As well, the annual Easter-egg hunts and Christmas concerts attracted up to sixty-five children from nearby villages. To accommodate the many families, and to provide berths for trading vessels, the government built a dock in Owen Bay in the late 1950s.

A few years later, Owen Bay was virtually deserted. The Schiblers had sold their property, and there was only a caretaker to look after some of their logging equipment and buildings that were left behind.

I travelled to Owen Bay in 1964 aboard our yacht, the *Kelea*, the year before leaving on our trip around the world. As we entered the bay, I sensed a strange atmosphere about me.

Above left: Pearl Schnarr and her pet baby female cougar, one of three orphaned cougars adopted by the three Schnarr girls.

Above right: An afternoon tea party at the Walters homestead at the head of Owen Bay in the 1930s. Some of those present besides the Walters are Mr. and Mrs. Logan Schibler, Mrs. Case and John Vanderest.

George Parsons' Flying Spray, in front of the Schibler home, Owen Bay.

Above: Gus Clements rowing with his wife Helen (nee Schibler). Sheila Cochran is at the bow. The mill in the background is near where my family's float house was once moored.

Right and below: Moving Day, Owen Bay, 1938. Note that the house is built on skids and is winched onto a raft. It would have been towed to a new location and probably winched back on land.

Perhaps it was because I was returning for the first time as an adult, or maybe it was the sight of vultures devouring an animal carcass on the small island by Boat Pass. We tied up to the government dock for the night and left the following morning. We saw no one, and no one appeared to be living there at the time.

The next time I heard about Owen Bay was a decade later, after returning from our ocean voyage. We were distressed to learn that our friends Alex and Margaret Cameron, also ocean voyagers, were reported missing in Owen Bay. Alex and Margaret had sailed their yacht *Drifter* to the South Pacific where they cruised for several years. When they returned to BC, they took the caretaker's job in Owen Bay, with the idea of building another boat in their free time. The plan never materialized.

Boating friends who came into the bay one day found the *Drifter* tied to the government dock and the log book filled out up to that afternoon. But there was only the mournful mew of the Camerons' cat to welcome them aboard. A search turned up an overturned dinghy, but Alex and Margaret were never seen again nor were their bodies ever found.

A few years later the name Owen Bay came up again, while I was interviewing someone for my "Offshore People" column in *Pacific Yachting*. I had been forewarned by a friend that the man I was going to interview had an unusual ghost story to tell. When I had finished the interview, I asked him about it. He told me that he really didn't believe in ghosts, but that an unexplained occurrence in Owen Bay had left him reconsidering his beliefs. With a strange expression on his face, he proceeded to tell me what had happened.

"My boat was one of six tied to the government dock that evening. I still have trouble believing that it actually happened, but during the night one by one the people on the other boats started their engines, untied their vessels and moved to the head of the bay. To tell the truth I really couldn't figure out what was going on. It's crazy to be leaving your moorage in the middle of the night. My cruising companion agreed as we watched the last boat leave the dock. It was a very dark night but the stars were as bright as I've ever seen them.

"I went back to bed feeling there was something spooky about the place. Shivering, I pulled the blankets over my head. It was so quiet I could have heard a pin drop. Then suddenly we heard someone walking on the deck right above our head. 'Who in the hell is that?' I shouted. No one answered, and when we looked out there was no one there.

"We went back to bed but couldn't sleep. Then, sure enough, there were footsteps again. This time we got up and searched the dock thoroughly, but there was no one to be seen. At that point we decided to ignore the intruder and went back to bed, and once again

Looking northwest through the entrance to Owen Bay. Haro Island is in the distance.

pulled the blankets over our heads, stuffing part of them in our ears hoping to shut out any sounds.

"There wasn't much hope of that as suddenly there was a great clanging noise on the deck. Something was picking up the boom chains we had found that day and dropping them on the foredeck over our heads. We jumped out of bed and practically collided in the companionway in our hurry to get on deck. Yet when we got there, there was no one to be seen. This time we also started our engine, untied our lines and moved to the head of the bay."

His mention of boom chains recalled to me with a start a conversation I had overheard long ago between my mother and father. They were talking about two men whose bodies had been dragged out of the nearby waters. The bodies had boom chains wrapped around them. (A boom chain weighs about a hundred pounds and is used to chain a boom together.)

The subject of Owen Bay surfaced again several years later in the summer of 1979, while I was cruising aboard the *Jubilee* in Desolation Sound. I was talking to an American couple about anchorages in the area. When they mentioned Owen Bay, I half jokingly asked them if they had seen any ghosts and they looked uncertainly at each other. Then the man told me that his wife thought she had seen someone lighting a candle in the small shed near the dock, but no one was there when they looked. Hesitating, he continued: "And when we turned in, we heard the creaking of oarlocks as if someone was rowing towards us through the darkness—but the sound never got closer."

In 1981, the *Jubilee* was tied dockside in

Above: Grandpa Schnarr with air wheel, Surge Narrows, 1953.

Lloyd Vaughan holding several dead marten caught in a trapline.

Above left: Jack and Ella Schibler's son Don. A net loft and a mill are in the background. Owen Bay, 1957.

Above right: The sailing vessel Jubilee *at the government dock in Owen Bay. I revisited many coastal villages aboard the* Jubilee.

A shack on the beach was all that was left of the old Schibler house at Owen Bay in 1989. Even the once-spiffy government dock had mostly disappeared.

Owen Bay, and I was happy to see that the community seemed to be coming back to life. There were a number of lodges scheduled to be built where the old homesteads had once been, and one man I talked to was building a beautiful log cabin that he planned to name "Ghost Bay Lodge".

A couple of years later, we dropped by again. Aside from a couple of power boats tied alongside the dock, Owen Bay seemed abandoned. "Ghost Bay Lodge" had been built, but the doors were locked and there was no one around.

After my article on Owen Bay appeared in *Pacific Yachting* in 1983, a number of people came forward to tell me their experiences when moored at this fabled government dock. One well-known sailing/cruising yachtsman had this to say. "My wife and I decided to get away over the Christmas season, to be some-

where quiet and by ourselves, so we took on some stores and headed towards Desolation Sound, going through Surge Narrows and the Okisollo Channel to Owen Bay, where we tied dockside. There was no one else around and it seemed like just a wonderful way to spend a few days. Before dinner that afternoon I went for a walk, and had only got a few feet past the old cabin when I noticed there were huge footsteps in the soft earth!" "How big?" I asked. "Oh, about a size 17 or 18 — not a normal-sized shoe! That night for the very first time in British Columbia, we locked up the boat before going to bed."

In the summer of 1988, my husband and I went cruising on the coast with our friend Ybo LaLau aboard the *Jubilee*. Toward the end of the holiday we dropped by Owen Bay. It was early evening and the little dock space there was had already been taken, so instead we an-

The bank where a meteorite once landed.

An old lifeboat, abandoned by its owner, is left to deteriorate on the beach at Owen Bay.

chored out. It was a peaceful enough night and the next morning when some of the other boats left we moved dockside. At first there was no one around. Then we met the owner of "Ghost Bay Lodge." We walked with him through the grassy meadows sprinkled with wild daisies and thistle to have a look at the lodge, which was ready to welcome guests. But he told us that his plans had changed and instead of operating a resort he was going to sell out and move to Belize. Nor did he give us any particular reason.

He did bring us up to date on what was happening around the bay, He said there were plans to develop other properties, but as yet nothing had got started. He also talked about some of the drifters who had come and gone.

"There is one man who calls himself the 'caretaker and wharfinger' who lives in a tree-house somewhere in the woods. Occasionally he'll appear and offer for sale some of the apples from the old fruit trees and try and collect moorage from the boats tied dockside. The big German shepherd dog you see roaming around belongs to him.

"There is another man who lives in a lean-to on that boat you see anchored out. He used to have a friend that lived here, that owned the old boat at the dockside. He was murdered— thrown off the stern of the ferry heading for Nanaimo when it went into reverse leaving Horseshoe Bay. He must have been travelling with the wrong crowd!"

Owen Bay does indeed seem to have some bad karma to work out. Some of the old tow-boat skippers I have spoken to agree there is something strange about that part of the coast. "You just feel it in your bones," said the late Micky Balotti. Bill Wolferstan observes in his cruising guide *Desolation Sound*, "An ominous feeling pervades the bay!"

The old mill is idle and casts a gloomy reflection in the water.

10. Big Bay • Stuart Island

Stuart Island was named after Captain Charles E. Stuart, an officer with the Hudson's Bay Company. It lies about 130 miles north of Vancouver at the entrance to Bute Inlet. The Yuculta Rapids lie to the west in the channel between Stuart Island and Sonora Island. The channel is part of the main north-south route between the south coast and Alaska. It provides an alternative route to Seymour Narrows, and is used by many of the smaller vessels.

Fishing boats at The Landing, Stuart Island, 1930s.

The island was known as a fishing centre long before the turn of the century, when oarsmen in small open boats travelled northward along the coast in search of land and a new way of life. When they reached Stuart Island, they stopped at the small cove near the southern end called "The Waiting Place" to rest their weary bodies and wait for slack water before proceeding through the rapids.

It was a rule of thumb for the early settlers to leave "The Waiting Place" forty-five minutes before the tide turned in the Yuculta Rapids, so they could reach Dent Island when the water was slack. The Dent Rapids are considered among the most dangerous rapids on the coast.

It was the end of the nineteenth century before the first Europeans began moving to Stuart Island. Attracted by the good fishing, they staked out land in the sheltered bays, built houses of timber cut nearby, and settled in. By 1920, there were more than one hundred people living on the island.

Floathouses and shacks built along the beach were the usual living quarters. Life was a combination of simple pleasures and hard work. Most of the families had goats, chickens and a vegetable garden. Fish supplemented their diet as well as their income.

The problem of fishing offshore in the rapids was solved in an ingenious way by a retired ship's master, Captain Watts. He built a fishing ramp on hinges that could be swung out over the rapids. He also used the flow of the rapids as sanitary disposal, building two outhouses at the end of what is now known as Watts Point, first dubbed "Shithouse Point" by towboat crews. The ramp had to be taken down eventually, as it interfered with tows going through the Pass.

Anderson Secord, who moved from Bute Inlet to Big Bay in 1907, was one of the first settlers. Others who pioneered the area were Henry Asman (Asman Point), William Muehle, the Smith brothers, Kellsey Moore (Kellsey Point), Jimmy Judd (Jimmy Judd Island), Gunner Swang, Buck Lewthwaite, Len Hatch, and the Stickland, Lansell and Squire families.

The property around "The Waiting Place" was owned by George Bruce, and became known as Bruce's Landing. Bruce was the storekeeper and postmaster, as well as fish and fur buyer. His competitor was Henry Ives, who had a floating store tied to Bruce's Landing. Henry's store was for the fishermen, and he would hire a boat to tow his store to wherever the salmon were running.

The Matt Gerard family bought the store and landing from George Bruce. They sold it to J.B. Willcock in the late 1920s and moved to Big Bay. The Willcocks were the storekeepers for the next twenty years.

I first saw "The Landing" at Stuart Island from the deck of the Union Steamship *Cardena* in the early 1940s. There was a magical feeling about the place as I looked down on the dock crowded with people milling around. Steamboat day was the social event of the week. No one wanted to miss it and some travelled many miles in small open boats to be there. They came not only to pick up mail and supplies but to meet their neighbours, hear the gossip and see who was new in town.

My attention was caught by the native Indian women who had come over from the Church House Reserve on the mainland side of Calm Channel. They were dressed in brightly coloured satin gowns with scarves holding back their shiny black hair. There were emerald green and purple gowns and red or golden scarfs. How I wished I could look like that!

My next visit to Stuart Island was several years later. I was nine years old and I felt very privileged that I was considered old enough to join my two older sisters, Edith and Louise, on a three-week fishing trip during summer holidays.

We rowed from our homestead on northern Quadra in two fourteen-foot clinker-built boats, making the trip in two stages, in order to navigate the Okisollo Rapids and the ones in the Hole-in-the-Wall during slack tide. The first stage took us to Etta Point at the southwestern entrance to the Hole-in-the-Wall. There we pulled the boats onto the rocks above the high tide mark, rested on a mossy bank and waited for slack water before continuing.

On a full running tide the rapids in the Hole-in-the-Wall average somewhere between twelve and fourteen knots, with giant whirlpools taking up most of the pass. While we watched, a huge snag about thirty feet long was pulled into the rapids and swallowed by a whirlpool. Several minutes later it shot out of the water at an enormous speed as though fired from a gun. Certainly neither of our boats or ourselves would have survived such an experience.

If you are lucky enough to see the rapids in the Hole-in-the-Wall from the shore at night, as we did when we were living in Owen Bay, you'll experience a strange phenomenon as the giant whirlpools and tremendous turbulence created by the swift running current are illuminated by phosphorus, casting an eerie, shadowy glow over the land.

Above: "The Waiting Place," Stuart Island, long ago.

Left: Tommy Thomas, a Welsh sea captain, sailed from Wales as a young man. Later he lived in Big Bay on a float house, and his sidekick Judd Engles lived on a boat tied alongside. This picture was taken in 1938.

Below: The Landing at Stuart Island, where rowers once waited for the tide at the Yuculta Rapids and Dent Island before continuing.

The Hole-in-the-Wall separates Sonora and Maurelle islands. At the western entrance near Okisollo, where the channel is narrow, the current will run up to sixteen knots on a full running tide, with giant whirlpools spanning the channel. (George McNutt photo)

Below: Picnic off Arran Rapids in the 1930s. Corrine Innes (in white by the water), Jack Innes (looking down), Gilbert Krook (bare back showing), Muriel Chapman (blond hair), Marge Innes (far right with white bow in hair).

Altogether it took seven hours to make the one-way trip to the small bay north of Parrish's Point where we found lodging in the abandoned Stickland house. The house had a door, but the glass from the windows was missing. It was built near the beach with a dock out front where we could tie our boats. There was a strange feeling about the place. Once a full-grown black bear came to the doorway, looked

at us and walked away. On several occasions during the night the rooms were flooded with light, yet there was no electricity. Locals called it the "Haunted House."

At Stuart Island we trolled for salmon in the evening before the turn of the tide. Every third day of the trip, one of us had a boat to ourselves. I can clearly remember my first turn. My sister Edith explained in detail where to fish and how to bring a salmon in if one took my line. We used green manila fishing lines with washboard flasher lures, and had a pot of live herring tucked under the seat to prevent them from jumping out.

With the the flasher and herring over the side and the line tied to my leg trailing behind, I began rowing gently through the water, imagining that a very large fish was swimming after the hook. It seemed like a very long time before I got a strike. It felt like a big one and I remembered my sister's instructions; when the fish is running give it extra line, when the line goes slack start pulling it in. Soon the big salmon was swimming alongside the boat. It was then I made my mistake. I got so excited that I forgot what Edith had told me and tried pulling the salmon in over the side of the boat rather than lifting it in. Sure enough, it dropped off and swam away!

What a disappointment! As the current had started to run there wasn't much time left for fishing. My sisters were waving at me to come in. Pretending not to see them, I quickly re-baited the hook, put the line back in the water and began trolling. Rowing was more difficult as the current was now running, pulling me toward the rapids. Just as I was about to give up, another fish took my line. This time I got it in the boat and with great pride rowed in to the fish-scow anchored in Parrish's Bay. I watched as the fish buyer weighed my salmon. It was a thirty-pound white spring that netted me seventy-five cents.

Salmon were plentiful in those days, with an average evening's catch being three and four salmon per line. That summer I earned enough money to buy a Baby Brownie camera for one dollar and kept myself supplied with chocolate bars and ice cream from Willcock's store at the Landing. I thought about that first camera many years later in 1977, after winning the Lens & Shutter travel-slide competition and a trip for two to Europe. Along with writing, taking pictures has become part of my life's work.

Many people have felt the magic of fishing near the swift-running tides off Stuart Island. The late Francis Dickie wrote the following in the March 20, 1946, issue of the *Family Herald and Weekly Star*: "Inshore along the entire length of the 200 yards of little bay the row-boats have appeared. From every home of the few settlers on these sheer shores is at least one member of the family with a handline weighted with from one to three pounds of lead. Among the local commercial fishermen the occasional visiting 'Sport' is conspicuous with rod and reel.

"Dusk is rapidly deepening. A few yards from each other the boats move very slowly, one to two persons to a boat, one rowing, the other fishing. Occasional greetings are exchanged. Even these are low voiced. For the most part all is very quiet, even the dark water stilled by the slack of the tide. Everyone is a little tense. No matter how long or often one has fished here the sense of waiting grips, that poised-to-pounce instinct deep within all despite civilization's thousand refining years."

While the rapids around Stuart Island were rich fishing grounds, they were also a source of tragedy. Two early families bereaved by the rapids were the Chapmans and the Inneses.

The Chapmans were among the first families to settle in Big Bay. Reg Chapman travelled in a small boat from Vancouver to Stuart Island in 1917 looking for suitable land to homestead. He found a section beyond Big Bay, near the Arran Rapids and Turnback Point, on the the way to Bute Inlet. Once he had secured the land, he married his sweetheart Dorris Dingle, a young English woman, in Vancouver. A few months later they sailed to Stuart Island, their small yacht loaded down with supplies.

Like most of the early settlers, they lived in

a tent while they were building their house. Their cookstove and heater was a four-gallon gas can. Reg Chapman had never worked in the woods before and had not learned to direct the fall of a tree by undercutting. The first big one he cut down landed on their tent—which, fortunately, was empty. Reg was an innovative man and later built a fishing ramp on hinges, like that of Captain Watts. The Chapman's first child, Stuart, named after the island, was born in 1919. Iris was born in 1923, Grace in 1925 and Muriel in 1931. Two weeks before each birth, Mrs. Chapman boarded a Union Steamship boat and travelled to Vancouver for the delivery. Two weeks after the baby was born, she was back home on Stuart Island.

By the end of the 1920s, the first school had opened in Big Bay. Stuart Chapman was one of the two boys and his sister Iris was one of the seven girls who made up the class. The school attracted other families who wanted to educate their children. Happy and Lydia Innes and Bert and Mae Brimacombe were some of the people who moved there so that their children could attend school. The Gerard family

Above: The Arran Rapids.

Left: Japanese fisherman Sigaru Matsunaga at Stuart Island, 1939.

Below: Japanese fishing fleet, Parrish's dock, Stuart Island, 1930s.

Above: Jack Schibler at Bute Inlet, 1940.

Below: Machine shop and floats at Parrish's Bay, Stuart Island, 1930s. Donald Innes is aboard the troller Doris S.

Stuart Island Landing from "The Bluff," 1939.

also relocated in Big Bay, after they sold the store and landing at "The Waiting Place" to the Willcocks.

Stuart Chapman drowned in the Arran Rapids in 1968. He and his wife were living on the old homestead when it happened. Stuart was a fisherman, but also worked with the Department of Highways. The day he went missing he told his co-workers that he didn't feel well and would have to go home. They watched him head down to his boat and he seemed to be doing okay. The next day his boat was found floating upright with empty gas tanks, but Stuart was never seen again. People speculated about what might have happened: maybe he stood up to change the gas tanks and fell overboard, or maybe he had a heart attack. No one will ever know. His widow continued to live at the homestead for many years after his death.

Happy and Lydia Innes moved their floathouse from Frederick Arm to Big Bay in 1930. They had four children—Marjorie, Bob, Corine and Jack—aged seven to three. Like other families on the coast, the Inneses logged, fished and raised their children. Through hard work and determination, life eventually became easier.

In 1938, they bought the hull of a thirty-foot boat and finished off the deck and cabin, using a steamer to bend the planks and hand tools for finishing work. The children helped, scraping the boards shiny smooth with broken glass. They called their new boat the *Inverness.* She was rigged as a troller. It was a big step forward for the Innes family as they now had a gasboat to go trolling for salmon instead of a rowboat for cod fishing. They eventually turned to logging, and it was through this industry they prospered.

In the early 1950s, tragedy struck the Inneses as a result of living near the rapids. Their youngest son Donald was home from school during Easter vacation. He decided to work in a logging camp to earn money to pay for a car. When vacation was over, he joined his brother Bob in an open boat on a trip to Ramsay Arm to pick up Bob's wife and newborn son, and somewhere along the way they came to grief. No one will ever know what happened. Some say they may have taken the shortcut through Canoe Pass between Sea Lion Rock and Sonora Island in the Yucultas. The boat was found floating upside-down, but Bob and Donald were never seen again. The shortcut has been named Innes Pass in memory of the two brothers.

The Inneses and the Chapmans offer two examples of what it is like to raise a family near dangerous tidal waters. Stuart Chapman and Bob and Donald Innes were experienced boating people who knew the rapids as well as anyone.

Today Stuart Island has changed a lot. Fishing is now a multi-million dollar business, with fishing lodges occupying the land where the old homesteads once stood. People fly in from all over the world to stay in one of the posh resorts. Instead of taking a rowboat to catch fish at the turn of the tide, they hire an expert guide. The Brimacombe's son Terry and his wife, Lu, own and operate their well-

Left: Brimacombe Fishing Resort, Big Bay.

Below: Boaters will find safe moorage in the community of Big Bay, where there is a store, pub, showers and laundry facilities. There is also moorage at the government dock centre and at Brimacombes Fishing Resort at far right. Looking northwest from the summit of Mt. Muehle, 1,710 feet, there is an excellent view of the rapids and Jimmy Judd and Gillard islands. To the northeast is Bute Inlet with lofty peaks to 8,000 feet. (George McNutt photo)

known Brimacombe Fishing Resort, where the old homestead used to be.

The really wonderful things about Stuart Island will never change, like the magic of living near the ocean where the current is always moving, where the misty air smells of kelp and the gulls can be heard in their fight for fish, over the distant roar of the rapids on a full tide. Those are the memories I will always treasure.

11. Read Island · Evans Bay · Surge Narrows

Read Island is separated from Cortes by two miles of water, and less than a mile of water lies beween Quadra and the western side of Read. Yet the history of each of these islands and the life of the people who have settled them, has been different. It seems that islands and villages, like individuals, have their own karma which they must work out.

Read Island has had a history of violence from the very beginning. Some say it started with an Indian massacre. Long ago, a marauding Kwakiutl tribe crept inland from Evans Bay. They took the small band of Salish people who were living on Read Island by surprise, and wiped them out. The grassy fields at the foot of Mt. William were drenched in blood.

Evans Bay, where the Kwakiutl landed, was the first site of European settlement. The numerous small coves within it made it an attractive place to disembark. As well, it was only a short distance from Heriot Bay and settlements on Cortes Island. Alex Russell was the first of these newcomers. A timber developer, Russell pre-empted 600 acres of Crown Land on Read Island in 1883. This was just one of several grants Russell obtained on the islands for the purpose of logging. Settlers who followed him were mainly farmers and fishermen, people who had come to work the land. By 1893, there were about sixty people living

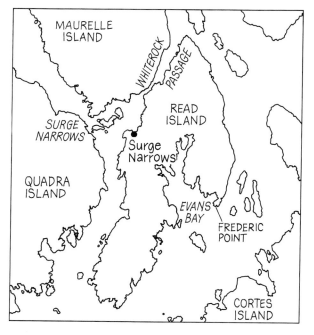

on the island, including storekeeper Peter Schuffer and farmers Richard Davis, Joseph Silva, Frank Willmot and John Smith.

One unusual fact is that thirty of the early settlers—half of the island's population—came from the Badlands of North Dakota. They included a number of characters of doubtful reputation. The story goes that this group of men were only a few steps ahead of the law when they crossed the border into Canada. Their troubles became part of the Read Island "karma."

Jack Myers, also known as Bart Mackenzie and Ben Kennedy, belonged to this group of Badlanders from North Dakota. He apparently had no intention of working the land for a living. Myers was planning quite a different lifestyle. He remained on the island just long enough to put together a money-making plan; then he returned to Vancouver where he bought a twenty-four-foot sloop and sixty cases of stolen whisky for two dollars a case. Travelling with him was his small dog, Blackie.

Myers's plan was to bootleg the whisky to the workers at Taylor's logging camp, where he knew the liquor would be in demand. The camp was working out of White Rock Bay, on the northwest side of Read Island. It was a wet, soggy afternoon on Friday, June 24, 1893, when Myers pulled into the Taylor camp. The men were just coming out of the woods, and when they spotted him, they went directly to the boat. The group included Salem Hinckly, the camp manager, and loggers Angus Cameron, Jim Burns, Jack O'Conner and John O'Neil. They were all eager to get their hands on the booze, especially when Myers told them the price—just two dollars a bottle. Together they bought two dozen bottles, and headed over to the bunkhouse to begin pouring drinks.

The weekend drinking party lasted from Friday night until early Monday morning. By this time everybody was drunk, and some were itching for a fight. Myers chose this moment to begin bragging about his dog. "Blackie'll let no one lay a hand on what's mine," he bragged, throwing his waistcoat to the floor and commanding the dog to guard it. When O'Conner took a dive for the coat, poor Blackie was terrified, and ran under one of the bunks. This infuriated Myers. He drew one of his pistols and began firing at the dog.

O'Conner intervened—and found the gun pointed at him!

The argument ended with O'Conner fatally wounded. The other men, who had been outside (or so they claimed), came rushing in when they heard O'Conner cry out. Myers told them it was an accident and threatened to kill anyone who wouldn't support his claim of innocence. It was a sobering moment. They looked at their dead friend on the floor, blood oozing from his chest, then covered the body with a blanket from one of the bunks.

Hinckly, the only one who was still relatively sober, took a boat and rowed across Sutil Channel to Cortes Island where Michael Manson, the local magistrate, was living. Manson accompanied Hinckly back to the Taylor camp, where he examined the body of Jack O'Conner to determine the cause of death. Myers stood by armed with a .44 Winchester rifle and two revolvers. He bragged of being one of Jessie James' gang, and said there was a warrant out for his arrest in the United States. He threatened to shoot Manson if he tried to arrest him. Manson, like the surviving loggers, was unarmed. He simply told Myers he needn't worry if he was innocent, and left to initiate legal proceedings.

A report of the shooting was sent to the provincial court office at Comox, where an autopsy was held. Michael Manson and the men from Taylor's camp were witnesses. When the inquiry was over, a warrant was issued for Myers' arrest, along with a $500 reward.

The murder made headlines in many BC newspapers, and it seemed only fitting that a police posse be sent out to capture the criminal. Seventeen men left Comox aboard two government vessels, *Estelle* and *Joan*. By the time they arrived at Read Island, Myers had taken Blackie, and his guns and ammunition, and vanished in his sloop.

The searchers spent several days scouring Calm Channel and Ramsey Arm. Then, as they headed into Bute Inlet, they saw a wisp of smoke drifting up through the trees. They apprehended Myers roasting venison over a campfire. He claimed to have been half-starved and out of ammunition when he had eaten Blackie the week before. Myers' trial was held in New Westminster. The jury found him guilty of manslaughter and he was sentenced to life in prison.

Life around Evans Bay went back to normal. With the Union steamship *Comox* making a twice-weekly call, new settlers were moving in. Among them was Edgar Wylie and his wife. The Wylies were New Yorkers who had travelled across the continent by stagecoach. They built the Wylie Hotel and trading post in Burdwood Bay, on Read Island. The first post office on the Island was opened in the hotel in 1893, with Edgar Wylie as postmaster.

About a year after Myers was sentenced to

life behind bars, the newspapers of British Columbia had another front-page story featuring the violent lifestyles of Read Islanders. This time a dead body was found in the bottom of a skiff adrift in Sutil Channel. A couple of loggers heading for work found the skiff and towed it and the corpse to Burdwood Bay. Edgar Wylie identified the corpse as Chris Benson, a partner of his in the store. John Smith, a friend of Wylie, suggested that Benson might have suffered a heart attack and injured the side of his face when he fell.

Again Michael Manson, justice of the peace from Cortes Island, was called in. By this time Manson was becoming something of a detective. He knew Benson's death was not accidental. Not only were the injuries to his face too severe, but there was no blood in the skiff. After making a thorough examination, Justice

Its light current makes Whiterock Passage an easier route for small craft than the fast-flowing Surge Narrows.

The head of Toba Inlet.

Aerial view over Frederic Point on Read Island, looking northwest up Whale Passage. (George McNutt photo)

Manson placed Benson in a rough coffin and took him to Vancouver aboard the *Comox*. There he had Dr. Bell-Irving, the city coronor, perform an autopsy, which concluded that the cause of death was homicide. Apparently Benson had been struck several times on the head and chest with a blunt instrument before he died.

After the autopsy, Michael Manson met with Chief Inspector Fred Hussey, of the Provincial Police in Comox, to discuss the case. Considering possible suspects, Manson ruled out Ed Wylie, who seemed truly shocked at Benson's death. Smith and his wife were unlikely suspects as they and the Bensons had been friends even before coming to Canada.

Manson believed the crime likely involved a woman, and there were only two to choose from: Mrs. Wylie, a quiet, reserved person, and Mrs. Smith, a rather talkative mother of four small children. Manson contracted a local fisherman, Bill Belding, to work undercover for him. Belding was to see what he could find out from Mrs. Smith. After several visits she confided that her husband had murdered

Chris Benson when he discovered that she and Chris were having an affair. The affair had been going on for a long enough time that a code of signals had been arranged. If Mrs. Smith had washing on the line, Benson knew the coast was clear. But the system wasn't foolproof: once, when Mrs. Smith thought her husband was going away for a few days, he returned unexpectedly, catching his wife and Benson. Smith became so enraged he clubbed Benson to death with a hammer, and set the body adrift in the skiff.

The trial was held in Vancouver, during the fall assizes of 1895, before the Honourable Mr. Justice Walkem. The defence lawyer was William J. Bowser, who later became the premier of British Columbia. Despite the strong evidence against Smith, the jury returned a verdict of not guilty. When he heard he was a free man, Smith went to the jury and began shaking hands. This infuriated Justice Walkem, who ordered Smith to leave the courtroom at once. He commented: "One does not like to see such a scene in a court of justice, as it might give rise to the suspicion that more than

Looking north up Hoskyn Channel from the deck of a yacht, with a spectacular panorama of the Coast Range in the distance.

goodwill had passed between the jury and accused!"

It was later learned that the Smiths were carrying on a two-sided affair. On his days away from home, John Smith was spending time with someone else's wife.

With the exception of the violent crimes, life on Read Island was much the same as in other turn-of-the-century coastal communities. The people who came to settle had the spirit of true pioneers. Moses Ireland, a well-known lumberman of the late 1880s, owned land at Evans Bay and later had a cattle ranch on Bold Point. He left his home in California when he was fourteen for the Cariboo Gold Rush, where he made a fortune. He was the kind of person who made and lost a lot of money in his lifetime, and knew a good deal when he saw one. He recognized that if he could buy land in British Columbia, timbered or untimbered, for a dollar an acre, there was money to be made. He borrowed money, invested it in timberland, held the land and then sold it after the price more than doubled.

The store and dock at Surge Narrows, with the Stafford cabin on the shore at right. The entrance to Whiterock Passage is just at the left of the photograph.

The wharf and store at Surge Narrows, late 1920s. The Tipton homestead is on the hill, and the small building beside the store was used as a schoolhouse.

The Tipton house, before the store was built. At upper left is an old barn and tool house, and the old school building is near the beach.

Ireland was a storyteller and a mystic with a great sense of humour. In 1905, he told a reporter from the *Province* newspaper that he'd seen a mysterious floating light that appeared like a woman in a flowing white gown. He felt it was a warning. Eight years later he was killed at his beloved homestead at Bold Point. His death remains an unsolved murder mystery.

The turn of the century saw many changes around Evans Bay. In 1905, the school that had started in the Wylie Hotel closed. Ed Wylie died three years later and was buried on a point near Bird Cove, in a crevice in a rock

that had an opening large enough for his body. The body and the crevice were covered with cement in which small stones were placed, spelling out "Ed Wylie 1908."

According to Walter MacLean and Bill Whittington, who bought the Wylie Hotel some years later, they found numerous bullets lodged in the planked walls during the renovations. However, no deaths were ever reported. "It's obvious, though, that it was no place for saints!" observed Whittington.

The southern end of the island, around Evans Bay, developed first, with the earliest store and post office, hotel and school. It was not until Robert Tipton and his wife, Margaret, moved to Surge Narrows in 1920, that the northern part of the island began moving ahead.

Robert Tipton, the son of a British millionaire cotton broker, and his wife had been given 238 acres of land at Surge as a wedding gift by Robert's father. After the honeymoon, the young couple decided to start their new life together in a new country and took up residence on their island property. It was relatively easy for Robert Tipton to move to a remote island along the coast, as he had seen service in the war and was accustomed to hard living. His wife, Margaret, on the other hand, had grown up in a mansion with maids and butlers, and had to adjust to a completely different lifestyle. To live in a shack without any amenities would be impossible for many women with her background, but she was of a hardy stock and took it all in her stride. She hung her fur coats and satin gowns in a closet, put her jewels aside and went to work alongside her husband, clearing and plowing the land.

Robert had assured his bride that he was destined to inherit some of his father's fortune and that within ten years they could return to an easier way of life. But that dream never materialized. When the British cotton market collapsed after World War I, his father lost his fortune. Margaret and Robert had no children of their own, but they adopted their niece, Winnifred, and nephews Clarence and Gary Keeling, who had been left homeless by the death of their parents. There were not enough school-age children on the island to qualify for a teacher, so as a temporary measure they hired a tutor to teach the Keeling youngsters and some other neighbourhood children. In 1925, they placed an advertisement in the *Province* that read: "Pre-emptions available for desireable settlers with children, without charge. Fertile coastal Island. Apply Box . . ." They received thirty-five replies. Some applicants became disillusioned when they learned how remote the area was, and that a rowboat was the main means of transportation. However, several families did come to settle, including the Redfords, Footes, Patersons, and

Wilsons. Among them there were enough children to qualify for a teacher.

Land for the school was donated by John Jones, the postmaster at Surge Narrows. His homestead was inland from the Union Steamship landing and was noted for its fine orchards and gardens. He was known as an eccentric and when his first house burned to the ground he made the next one virtually fireproof by building it out of cement and tin. The settlers built the schoolhouse themselves out of logs. The first teacher, Mabel Plommer, welcomed children to the new school in the fall of 1927.

For the next twenty years, Read Island continued to develop. Roads were built, cars were brought in and there was easy access to most parts of the island. Logging and fishing remained the main industries and—with the exception of an earthquake in 1946 that destroyed a lot of property—life was fairly prosperous.

However, as in other coastal communities, following World War II the population of the small villages decreased and by 1960 there were only a few families living on the island. Margaret and Robert Tipton were among the last to go. They had lived at Surge Narrows for forty-two years, acting as storekeepers, fishbuyers, Justice of Peace and friends to the needy. They were kind, generous people who were loved by those who knew them. Certainly I can remember them from the time we had our homestead on Quadra Island. A trip to Surge Narrows was a special trip out, and I can remember spending my collection of silver nickels there. Interestingly enough, when I returned many years later, I found a silver nickel on the pathway.

In 1957, the Tiptons sold their holdings at Surge to the Hopkins family. By that time there were only a few families left on Read Island. The schools had closed, and logging and fishing virtually ceased. The Hopkins family stayed at Surge Narrows for a couple of years, then sold their businesses to George and Marie Dodman, who ran the fuel docks, store and post office there for the next seventeen years. They might still be there had not Marie's health failed her.

Mernie Summers and Jean Brown, two Vancouver businesswomen, bought the business from the Dodmans. They ran it until 1981, and then closed the doors of the operation for the first time in fifty years and moved back to Vancouver. The few islanders who are living there feel stranded, without a post office, store, fuel docks or scheduled sea-plane service. From Jean and Mernie's point of view, however, it

Above left: The Tiptons' children: (left to right) Gary, Clarence and Win, with the family's team of horses, Dan and Bess.

Above right: Fishing boats at Tipton dock.

Left: Bob Tipton getting shellfish from small gut between Stuart and Gopel islands.

was a tough way to make a living. "You're on call twenty-four hours a day and have to be really dedicated in order to stick it out."

In 1986, the property was purchased by Jim Day of Seattle, who hopes to turn it into a resort some day.

Life around Evans Bay and Surge Narrows has changed since the early days. Fish farms have replaced the homesteads in many bays and inlets, as a new era of de-settlement is taking place. It seems that the island has worked out its violent karma and only peace remains as you walk along the winding trails that bypass old orchards, where blackberry vines and wild rose bushes compete for space along unseen fences.

Above: A deer, having just swum across Hoskyn Channel, rests beside George Stafford's cabin, built at Surge Narrows in the 1940s.

12. Shoal Bay

Once the most populous village on the coast of British Columbia, Shoal Bay on East Thurlow Island is situated on Cordero Channel, opposite Phillips Arm. It is about 130 miles north of Vancouver. Originally known as Thurlow, its gradually shoaling harbour suggested a new name for the village.

A beach strewn with seaweed and sand and pebbles glistening from the wash of the ocean covers most of the foreshore. A small river gently winds its way toward the sea. Beyond the high tide mark lie marshland, meadows and a densely forested valley. High mountains cradle the valley on either side, affording a sweeping view of the channels that lace the coastal islands. In the distance, glaciers and frosted mountain peaks extend toward the horizon as far as the eye can see.

People from all over the world came to Shoal Bay in the late 1800s in search of gold. The transient population at that time, believed to number around five thousand, boasted that the community was even larger than the new city of Vancouver.

By 1898, two hundred mineral claims had been registered in the district of Thurlow. Many were staked by small entrepreneurs, but several of the larger mines were owned by British Columbia Golds Limited, an English company, including the Dorth Morten and Alexandra mines on Phillips Arm, the Yuclaw and Puddle Dog mines on Channel Island, and the Douglas Pine mine on the steep slopes above Shoal Bay.

Before the gold rush, the district of Thurlow was a centre for commercial logging. People had lived there since the early 1880s, and one of the largest sawmills on the coast operated at Shoal Bay. The mill continued to work after the mines were open, and both industries used teams of oxen to haul sleds with cedar skids to bring their products to the harbour. Some of these old skids are still visible today, slivers of aged grey cedar in the heavy green moss.

View of Shoal Bay and dock, from the hill above.

Map of the planned townsite of Shoal Bay, 1894. The plan was never realized, and now Shoal Bay is virtually a ghost town.

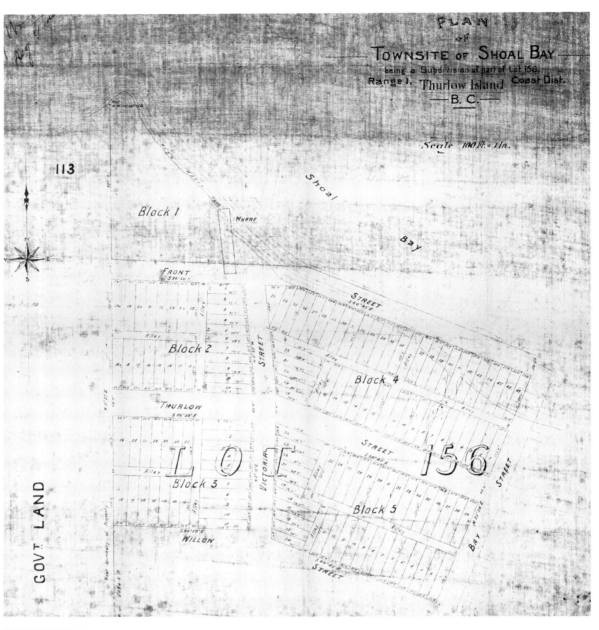

Estelle Germaine at Shoal Bay with the McDonald children, 1905. Estelle travelled across Canada by stagecoach.

Once the material reached the harbour, it was loaded onto barges near shore. Tugs then towed the barges to smelters at Vanada on Texada Island, to Everett, Washington, or to the Dorth Morten cyanide plant on Phillips Arm. Lumber also was shipped out via tug and barge, either to Vancouver or other large centres along the coast.

Panhandlers, miners, loggers, fishermen and trappers were all part of the early settlement at Shoal Bay. It was a boom town, with three hotels, a post office, a general store and more than one brothel to serve the large transient male population.

The harbour was always a hive of activity. Rowboats and canoes were pulled up on the beach while larger vessels lay at anchor; steam tugs with their barges came in several times a week to load ore and lumber; and boat day, when the Union steamship arrived, was especially busy. People from up and down the coast came to collect mail, pick up supplies and hear the latest news from Vancouver.

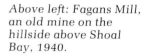

They left their boats on the beach, and sauntered down the floating gangway to the dock to socialize with their friends and await the arrival of the *Comox*. A holiday spirit prevailed and sometimes the boat-day gathering grew so large that the float was in danger of sinking.

In the late 1880s, John and Esther Ward and their two daughters, Mary Jane and Rose, towed their floathouse into this boom town. Shoal Bay seemed like paradise after the ordeal they had just endured.

Living in the outback was not new to them, and life thus far had been anything but easy. John, Esther and their family had moved to Vancouver from Winnipeg in search of free land. They were poor people who could neither read nor write, and to make life even more difficult, they were Irish. They felt that to be Irish in eastern Canada was worse than a sin, so they moved west in order to escape this prejudice.

When they arrived in Vancouver, they booked into a cheap hotel in Gastown where they met other families also looking for free land. None of them had any idea what the coast was like; when the government agent offered them land at the head of Knight Inlet, telling them it was to be the northern terminus of the Canadian National Railway, it seemed too good to be true—and it was!

The families arrived at the head of Knight Inlet on a soggy wet day in June 1890. A cold north wind swept down the glacier, chilling them to the bone, and tents did little to keep out the cold night air. Forty men, women and children worked side by side clearing the land

and building log houses; it was of utmost importance to complete these before winter set in. They raised chickens, goats, and pigs; staples were brought in by a small boat once a month from Alert Bay, sixty miles away.

They settled in and waited for track to be laid to their doorstep. Seven years later a survey party came through and told them there would never be a railway built to that part of the coast. Disheartened, the families left. Some moved back to Vancouver, others resettled in other coastal areas. The Wards put their house on a float and took a tow to Shoal Bay.

When the Wards arrived in Shoal Bay, only

Above left: Fagans Mill, an old mine on the hillside above Shoal Bay, 1940.

Above right: The old dance hall at Shoal Bay. It was converted to a store after the original store burned.

Emily and Raymond Tarr paddling, Dick Jamieson (centre), 1947. Jack Morrison's house is in the background on the east side of Shoal Bay.

and men tipped heavily just for the pleasure of looking at them.

Shortly after the turn of the century, the Greenfields decided to sell. They had made a tidy sum in Shoal Bay and were ready to return to city life. When the Wards learned that the hotel was being sold, they pooled their resources and bought it. John, Esther, Mary Jane and Rose all took an equal share. The Thurlow Hotel continued to flourish under their ownership, and it wasn't long before the Ward family became wealthy.

After the Wards took over the hotel, a man by the name of Peter MacDonald arrived at Shoal Bay. Peter had a lust for gold, and an attraction for the good-looking Rose Ward. He was experienced in the hotel trade himself and owned the Bodega and Mansion hotels in Gastown. After meeting Rose, he decided to sell his hotels, buy out the shares that John, Esther and Mary Jane had in the Thurlow, and take up residence in Shoal Bay. Rose and Peter were married; after the wedding, Esther, John and Mary Jane moved to Vancouver.

For the next twenty-seven years, the MacDonalds were permanent residents of Shoal Bay. Besides running the post office, store and hotel, they cleared land, farmed and raised five children. Their first and only son was born in 1903, a year after they were married. The girls came along at irregular intervals: Rose was born in 1905, Eleanor in 1914, Lorna in 1920, and Barrie in 1925.

The sixteen-room hotel became a landmark in Shoal Bay. The rooms were usually booked

two of their four daughters were still with them. Their youngest daughter had died of tuberculosis in Knight Inlet and was buried at Alert Bay; the second eldest girl was deaf, and the church insisted that she be sent to a special school in Ontario.

With their floathouse tied near the beach, the family went to work for Peter Greenfield, owner and operator of the Thurlow Hotel. John worked as bartender, Esther and the two daughters worked in the kitchen and cleaned the rooms. It was quite a change from Knight Inlet. The family was grateful and knew how to work hard. The hotel was doing a booming business, whisky was cheap, and the men came in from the mines and logging camps to cash in their cheques and have fun. Rose and Mary Jane were good-looking young women,

Above: From the hillside above Shoal Bay there is a sweeping view of Phillips Arm and the spectacular Coast Range in the distance. Ybo LaLau enjoys the view.

Right: On the hillside above the bay are the remains of old, moss-covered buildings, 1984.

by people in transit in small boats or on the Union Steamship. The large, airy dining room with a view of the bay was kept busy with the hotel guests, and with people coming to shop or visit. The real money-maker was the bar. Even though some of the mines had closed down and the sawmill wasn't operating, the men still liked their whisky and came to the hotel to drink. In the early years of the century, the "house special" for whisky was two drinks for twenty-five cents. Peter and Rose spent a lot of time at the hotel keeping an eye on things. When someone drank too much and became rowdy, he was asked to leave.

One night in the spring of 1919, they had a real problem with a regular who was trying to pick a fight. He was finally thrown out. Drunk and angry, he set fire to the hotel, then disappeared, never to be seen again. Within minutes the old hotel was a raging inferno. People were screaming and running for their lives. In her struggle to save some of her personal possessions, Rose MacDonald was badly burned. The next day, cinders were all that was left of the colourful establishment. Fortunately, no one died in the blaze.

Because they were uninsured, it was a big loss for Peter and Rose. Without the booming trade of the previous decade, the cost of rebuilding was out of the question. They continued to operate the store, post office and fuel docks and maintained the government

wharves. But they never recovered from the loss of the hotel.

In 1927, the MacDonalds sold out to C.C. Thompson, who ran the operation until after World War II. Some old-timers say that C.C. Thompson was the best storekeeper on the coast. He not only stocked the shelves with every imaginable item, but he never refused a request for food if someone came in hungry.

Above: Shoal Bay Lodge, rebuilt in the 1960s. The ironwood pilings, foreground, were installed in 1927.

Below: The sailing vessel Jubilee is tied dockside at Shoal Bay in late September.

He often loaned money to coastal residents who were down and out. Being generous was probably his downfall. In 1945, finding that his debts were larger than his credits, he put the store up for sale.

Raymond Tarr become the new owner. Tarr had moved to the coast from California and was living in a log cabin in Loughborough Inlet when the business in Shoal Bay came up for sale. He bought the land, buildings and store, not including the stock, for $5,000. Shortly after the purchase, he married Emily McGower, a native of Blind Channel. They worked hard at Shoal Bay, but luck wasn't with them. Three months after they opened the store it burned down. The fire was started by an overheated drum stove and within minutes was raging out of control.

Drum stoves were cheap and very effective heaters, but caused many fires along the coast. Buildings were usually of frame construction, cedar planked and lined with newspaper to keep out the drafts. If allowed to burn freely with their dampers open, the heaters turned red hot, creating an extreme fire hazard. Drum heaters were undoubtedly responsible for most of the fires that destroyed Shoal Bay's stores, hotels and a brothel over the years.

The store was rebuilt within a year, and the building still serves the visitors who stop in at Shoal Bay. The insurance, however, barely covered the stock on the shelves, so Raymond and Emily found it difficult to make a living. They continued in Shoal Bay until 1952, raising their two children to school age. The school in Shoal Bay, which had opened in 1910, had closed many years before. For that and other reasons, it seemed time for the Tarr family to move to a more populated area.

Shoal Bay was no longer the boom town of the late 1800s, but during the 1950s it was still a vital refuelling and provisioning depot for local people, and for small craft travelling Cordero Channel. Some of the people logging and living in the area at that time and using Shoal Bay facilities, were Roy Karlsson, Bill Baker, Len Hatch and Buck Lewthwaite, all well-known names along the coast.

Raymond Tarr remembers the day when he counted as many as ninety fishing boats tied alongside the wharf, waiting for the slack at Green Point Rapids farther up the channel. After 1945, aircraft began refuelling in Shoal Bay. Jim Spilsbury of Queen Charlotte Airlines was a regular customer, as was Carl Agar of Okanagan Helicopters, one of the pioneers in the field of helicopter design and construction.

Cecil Carrol and Gar Bergman and their wives bought the store and land. After a year, the Carrols decided that storekeeping was not for them, so they turned their shares over to the Bergmans, who ran the business until 1957. At that point, Shoal Bay was sold to Mrs. J. Dickie. But it wasn't an easy way to make a living, and when a group from Seattle offered to buy the land and build a lodge, Mrs. Dickie was only too anxious to sell.

The twenty-room lodge opened a few years later and is still in operation today, a quarter century and several owners after the last hotel closed. The government dock is still in good condition, thanks to the ironwood piers installed in 1927. Many boats still tie up and enjoy the spectacular view of Phillips Arm. Meals and drinks can be ordered at the lodge, and ice is available, but there is little else to be found in the way of supplies. The house that Ray and Emily built still stands, as does the store, on its pilings over the water. Nothing is left of the old orchard or of the homestead.

A walk through the surrounding forest brings you in touch with Shoal Bay's yesterdays. There are old log cabins tumbling to the ground, cedar skids, a donkey engine and an old Ford ambulance that was used back in the 1950s. (Recently the ambulance was restored and put back in service on Cortes Island.) On the hillside lie remnants of the old buildings of the Douglas Pine Mine, and warnings to be careful of gaping holes leading into the shafts. Other than these few relics, little remains as evidence of the five thousand people who once inhabited the area.

13. Blind Channel

Blind Channel is the name of a small protected harbour on the eastern side of West Thurlow Island. Mayne Passage runs by its front doorstep, connecting with Greene Point Rapids to the north and Discovery Passage to the south. Blind Channel was named by early navigators because, looking north or south along Mayne Passage, it appears to be blocked by land, and it is only when you continue along the channel that the opening appears.

Travellers en route from Discovery Passage to Loughborough Inlet, or destinations along Chancellor and Wellbore channels, used to stop at Blind Channel to wait for slack water before navigating Mayne Passage and the swift currents of Greene Point Rapids.

Besides waiting for the tide, travellers could take on supplies at a general store, and rest their weary bones at one of the local homes, where the cost of bed and breakfast might range from nothing to fifty cents a day.

The people who settled at Blind Channel near the turn of the century were loggers, prospectors, trappers, fishermen, and their families. The *British Columbia Directory* for 1910 lists nine lumbermen, six woodsmen, a blacksmith and a mill manager at Blind Channel. Native Indians, women and children were not listed in the directories of the time, but there were several of each in the village. In fact, there were enough children to support a school.

As the list of occupations suggests, most of the industry in Blind Channel was based on logging the magnificent stands of Douglas fir, cedar and spruce on East and West Thurlow islands. By 1910, large companies like the Thurlow Island Lumber & Sawmill Company had set up operations there.

To maintain some control of the timber cut, the British Columbia Forest Service had camps at Thurston Bay, Blind Channel and Roy. Thurston Bay, on Sonora Island, was where the Service kept most of its patrol boats and maintained a boatyard and repair shop. As many as ten families lived at Thurston Bay between 1910 and the early 1940s, when the camps were phased out.

In 1918, W.E. Anderson purchased a defunct sawmill on the foreshore at Blind Channel for the purpose of establishing a cannery and fish-packing plant. Anderson, who had

The village of Blind Channel in 1925. (CRM 11680)

Cecil Carrol's towboat company was moored at Greene Point. The colourful camp illustrates the zest for life that he maintained until his death in the late 1980s.

A few memories from a long-forgotten place on the coast.

made his money in the Klondike gold fields, owned the cannery at Quathiaski Cove. In order to expand his canning business, he had to set up a separate operation some distance away because each cannery had exclusive rights to all salmon caught within a designated territory.

Like its parent, the cannery at Blind Channel was named the Quathiaski Canning Company. The company not only ran a company town, but owned all the boats engaged to serve the cannery. Customers at the company store paid for merchandise with tokens they received for selling fish.

Once the cannery was running smoothly, Anderson and his partner, Frank Allen, built a large shingle mill adjacent to it. They also built a massive boiler room to supply power for both mills. It had thick concrete walls, double-lined with firebrick. (The diesel generators used to supply electricity for Blind Channel today are located inside the old boiler room to suppress the noise.) The same boiler room gave the community electricity for a few hours each evening. When the steam from the boilers ran out, the generator was kept going

by a pelton wheel, driven by water brought down the valley through a wooden pipe. When power from both these sources ran out, an old gas engine had to be cranked into life.

Important visitors to Blind Channel were the Columbia Coast Mission ships *Columbia* and *Rendezvous*. The mission was first conducted by the Rev. John Antle and later by Rev. Alan Greene. Services were held either aboard ship or on shore. If the service was on land, a portable organ named "Little Jimmy" was carried to the location.

At Christmas time the Coast Mission vessel travelled up and down the coast visiting villages and isolated logging camps and homesteads. I remember when Alan Greene, as Santa Claus, came to our homestead on northern Quadra to distribute parcels to all the family. If at all possible, no one went without a visit from the Mission at Christmas time.

When the cannery at Blind Channel closed down in the late 1930s, it was taken over by some Japanese Canadians who operated it as a fish saltery. However, when war with Japan broke out, the owners were taken away and placed in internment camps, and the saltery closed its doors forever.

Two well-known and typical residents of the Blind Channel area were Cecil Carrol and his wife Lillian. Their lives span the area's period of prosperity and its gradual decline. Cecil was born in Vancouver in 1916. When he was still a young boy, the family moved to Port Harvey where his father, Martin Carrol, was logging. The Carrols later towed the floating camp to a sheltered cove on the mainland near the junction of Cordero Channel and Mayne Passage. Cec Carrol's mother, Ada, was instrumental in starting the first school at Blind Channel. Cecil started school there in 1922, when he was six years old. At that time the one-room school had fourteen children in grades eight and nine.

According to Cecil, Blind Channel was a boom town in the 1920s. Besides the cannery and mill, there were tradesmen like Percy Sutherland, a first-class boat builder, and Bill Cowie, one of the best machinists on the coast. Both had more work than they could handle.

Cecil's wife, Lillian (nee Westbloom), was born in Halifax. Her family moved west in 1919, after losing most of their possessions in the Halifax Explosion two years earlier. The Westblooms lived with an aunt at Edgewood on the Arrow Lakes when they first came to British Columbia. They planned to stay with her only a couple of years until they got some money together, but Lillian's father died shortly after they arrived and Lillian and her mother stayed on. In 1922, Lillian and her mother travelled to Vancouver, and while visiting there her mother met Alex (Buck) Lewthwaite. They fell in love, were married and moved to Topaz Harbour where Alex was

Deadfall in the forest, Blind Channel.

A small house shaded by the forest is all that remains of an old homestead from the early years of this century.

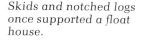

Skids and notched logs once supported a float house.

The general store and houses at Blind Channel in 1932. (Houghton-Brown Collection, CRM 6646)

working for the Wilson & Brady Logging Company. Like Cecil, Lillian grew up on floating camps at Jackson Bay and Read Bay and Loughborough Inlet.

Lillian met Cecil when the family travelled from Grays Creek to Loughborough Inlet to attend a Christmas concert. She was ten years old at the time, and he was twelve. "I was really impressed by his wonderful deep singing voice. I don't believe there was any deep feeling back then, but after that Cec came over to the house to borrow my comic books!"

The years Lillian spent in Granite Bay on Quadra Island working for Mrs. Clay Anderson was her favourite growing-up time. She helped Mrs. Anderson with the children, but there was plenty of free time, lots of young people to have fun with, and parties almost every week. "Granite Bay was a very special place," she reminisced. "It was almost landlocked and surrounded by high hills. In the winter time with the snow coming down over the beach, it looked like a Christmas card. One time when Granite Bay was completely frozen over we had to meet the Union Steamship by horse and buggy at the entrance to the bay!"

Cec came down to the dances at Granite Bay. They were always well attended, and it was a good opportunity to get to know each other better. On the coast in those days, you were picked up in a boat instead of a car, and unless you lived in the village where the dance was, the trip took several hours.

Cecil and Lillian were married and contin-

The sawmill and fish cannery started by W.E. Anderson in 1918 ceased operation in 1935. (Houghton-Brown Collection, CRM 6649)

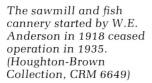

ued their life together on the coast. They started a towboat company in their bay north of the Greene Point Rapids. "A certain remoteness from big city life keeps people together. With life today that is a rare opportunity," said Lillian.

By the end of the 1940s, Blind Channel was slowing down. The cannery had closed, and the shingle mill had been destroyed by fire twice and was not rebuilt a second time. There weren't many jobs for the few settlers who remained. But the government dock was still there, as was a small store and restaurant, waiting to enter the next stage of Blind Channel's history.

Toward the end of the 1960s, the Richter family was doing some coastal cruising aboard their thirty-foot motor launch. They were running up Cordero Channel and decided to take a side trip to Blind Channel to pick up a loaf of bread. "It was raining heavily," recalled Phil Richter, "and we were surprised to see a good-sized government dock and a store, but hardly anything else. There was a For Sale sign on the store. We bought the bread and went back on the boat and began talking about buying the Blind Channel holdings."

Edgar, the father, was dissatisfied with his work as an engineer servicing aircraft engines at Vancouver International Airport, and was looking for a change. His wife, Annemarie, was not so keen to make such a radical change in lifestyles, but on a subsequent visit to Blind Channel on a clear, frosty winter day she changed her mind. The Richter family moved to Blind Channel in March 1970, determined to make it a tourist resort.

Annemarie's parents, known as Oma and Opa, moved up a few months later. Blind Channel is a family affair. Phil, the eldest son, and his wife Jennifer both work at the resort. His brother, Alfred, who works in the towing business, lives on Cordero Island, but Alfred's wife Leslie sometimes helps out at Blind Channel. Robert, the youngest son, also works at the resort when he is not away at school.

Both Edgar and Annemarie have found a new challenge in operating the Cedar Post Inn, a seasonal restaurant in their home. The name is suggestive of the "Thurlow Cedar" close by: a giant living tree, measuring approximately twenty feet in diameter at the highest point that a person can reach with outstretched arms. An attempt was made several years ago to drill to the core and determine the age of the tree, but the sampling drill was much too short. Educated guesses place the age of the Thurlow Cedar at about 2,500 years. The hike to the tree takes about twenty minutes and involves crossing the creek at the north side of the bay via a new footbridge. The Fletcher Challenge company has built an excellent forest interpretive trail to the big cedar and beyond.

The area around the Thurlow Cedar was

Above: Living in float house communities was common on the coast during the first half of the century. In some places it still is. Among the many advantages: plumbing is simplified, and firewood floats up to the front door.

Left: Today Blind Channel has up-to-date docking facilities with lodging, a restaurant, a general store and a bakery. Boaters are advised to make advance bookings during the summer months.

Below: A floating home anchored in a quiet bay can provide an inexpensive and secluded lifestyle. High-powered motor boats or seaplanes soon bring you back to civilization.

Saltwater lagoons, where the ocean seeps over the rocks at high tide, provide a home for many species of seabirds, and a warm bath for summer visitors.

logged in the past, and it is not clear why this giant was spared. The size of the nearby stumps of first growth indicates, however, that the loggers were not using equipment that could have handled the tree. BC Forest Products Ltd., which holds the tree farm licence here, has made a commitment to preserve the big tree for posterity. Standing in silence beneath such a large living tree is like being in a cathedral.

Travelling east on Nodales Channel.

Camp Cordero, a floating restaurant on Cordero Channel near Greene Point, began operation in the early 1980s and has been a big success. The owners are Reinholdt and Doris Kuppers. Boaters are advised to make bookings well in advance.

14. Hardwicke Island

Hardwicke Island lies about 140 miles north of Vancouver. It is separated from the mainland to the east by Sunderland Channel and to the southeast by Wellbore Channel. York Island, an army base during World War II, is off the northern tip of the island. The windswept Johnstone Strait, with Helmcken Island in midstream, separates Hardwicke from Vancouver Island.

Named by Captain Vancouver in 1792 for Philip Yorke, third Earl of Hardwicke, the island measures approximately fifteen miles long and seven miles wide. The main village is on the western side of the island opposite Kelsey Bay. Earl Ledge, a rocky reef, extends about a mile seaward from the village.

The village on Hardwicke looks out on the Inside Passage and a constant flow of shipping: cruise liners, tugs with a tow, fish boats and pleasure craft heading north and south along the coast. Waters between Hardwicke and Kelsey Bay are often turbulent, with fresh north winds funnelling down the channel. When a three- or four-knot current is running north against the wind, most small craft head for shelter!

The Salish people were the earliest recorded inhabitants of Hardwicke Island. They were driven off the island by the Lekwiltoks, a fierce branch of the Kwakiutl. The Lekwiltoks launched their final surprise attack from Topaz Harbour on the mainland east of the island. When the first European settlers arrived, the inhabitants of Hardwicke were Kwakiutl.

European settlement began with Jack Cook and his partner, Ben Rice, who began logging on Hardwicke near the turn of the century. Their camp was located on the foreshore behind Earl Ledge. The two men logged with cross-cut saws, then used a team of oxen to pull the timber out of the forest on a sled running on greased skids.

A Japanese outfit logging on Hardwicke around 1911 used teams of Clydesdale horses for hauling out the logs over the same cedar skids that Cook and Rice built. Their horses were treated with great respect, and during their New Year's celebration, a stack of good-luck rice cakes and oranges with burning candles were placed in front of each horse's stall. If the candles burned down, good luck followed. If they went out, some misfortune during the year was predicted for the animal. Perhaps most of the candles went out, since the horses were soon replaced by a steam-powered donkey engine!

William Kelsey and his family, who came to Hardwicke around the turn of the century, were the first permanent settlers on the island. They pre-empted 114 acres of land along the foreshore behind Earl Ledge. Kelsey had been hand-logging in Topaz Harbour and continued logging on Hardwicke. As well, he had a stand of timber to work on Vancouver Island, where he eventually moved.

A number of families have lived on Hardwicke Island since the turn of the century, including my own. All of them relocated to other parts of the coast. With one exception, that is. There has been at least one member of the Hans Bendickson family living on Hardwicke since the family moved there in 1918.

Hans Bendickson was a Norwegian by birth. He hand-logged on Quadra and Read islands, as well as in Jervis Inlet, before moving to Hardwicke. He had a floating camp and a small tug, the *Rex*, which towed the camp when he changed location. The camp was made up of several buildings, including the family's home and workshops. There were many floating camps on the coast at that time, including our own.

Aboard the camp were Mr. and Mrs. Bendickson and their seven children—Arthur, George, Barney, Harold, Fred, Jim and Lilly—who ranged in age from two to twelve years. The family moved ashore on Hardwicke, where they cleared and cultivated land and brought in livestock. With the Bendickson children and the three Kelsey girls, plus those of other families living on the island, there were enough children to qualify for a school. The original one-room school is still standing near the old Bendickson home.

Hans Bendickson had a good-sized timber lease on Hardwicke, which he logged for many years. As his sons grew up, they also turned their hands to logging, and the business, called the Bendickson Logging Company, became an extensive operation.

My family lived on Hardwicke Island for several years during the 1930s. My sister Inamar was born while my family lived there. My sister's birth was a race with the stork, as the saying goes. The only vessel available to take my mother to the hospital was the *Inamar*, owned by a visitor to the island, W.H. Malkin, then the mayor of Vancouver. The

The Bendickson family, gathered on the steps of their home. Standing (left to right): Arthur, George, Barney and Harold. Seated (left to right): Fred, Mr. and Mrs. Bendickson, Jim and Lilly.

nearest hospital was St. Michael's at Rock Bay, a twenty-mile trip down Johnstone Strait. Hans Bendickson, who was experienced in those waters, offered to pilot the vessel.

"We had the *Inamar* going full throttle," his son Harold recalled. "Mr. Malkin was nervous with his magnificent vessel travelling at that speed, but we insisted it was the only way we'd get to Rock Bay on time." My sister was born at the hospital shortly after they arrived. It seemed appropriate to my mother that she name her newborn daughter Inamar, after Malkin's boat.

My two older sisters, Edith and Louise, attended the one-room school on Hardwicke. Enda Cuthbert was the schoolteacher at that time. I went to school at Hardwicke when my family was living at our homestead on Quadra

Island. During that year I stayed with Mr. and Mrs. Bendickson Sr. in their wonderful old farmhouse.

When the Bendickson children grew up, some remained single while others married and settled on Hardwicke or other parts of the coast. Arthur, the eldest son, became president of Bendickson Logging when his father retired, and married the Enda Cuthbert who had taught school on Hardwicke.

Jim married Hazel Anderson from Hardwicke. He also had an active role in the family logging company. Jim and Hazel had a home on Hardwicke, as well as in Campbell River. Jim died in 1988. According to his brother Harold, "Hardwicke was a real tonic for Jim, and his personality changed as soon as he set foot on the island."

The Bendickson homestead on Hardwicke Island. The big house in the centre was built by Hans Bendickson in the 1920s. The one-room school my family attended is at back left. Bendickson Logging, now in the hands of the third generation, has recently logged in Port Neville Inlet. They plan to be back logging on Hardwicke someday.

Left: Looking across Hardwicke Island (middle) and Johnstone Strait into Kelsey Bay. (photo copyright Tim Poole)

Below: Moving on the coast was often a matter of towing your house along with you.

Fred and his wife Dorothy moved to Burnaby, where they lived until his death in the 1970s.

Barney had a towboat company based on the Fraser River. He lived in Vancouver until his death some years ago, and never married. George also stayed single and lived and worked at the homestead before moving to Vancouver.

Lilly married Olaf Hansen from Port Neville. The wedding, held in the old school house, was followed by speeches and dancing and a scrumptious Scandinavian smorgasbord at the Bendickson family home. It was one of the bigger weddings on the coast. Hundreds of friends turned out to celebrate the marriage of the Bendicksons' only daughter. Guests travelled from all parts of the coast by boat and plane. Some were ferried across the strait from Kelsey Bay in a sea-shuttle that the family had organized for the occasion. After the wedding, Olaf took his bride back to Port Neville, where they still reside.

Harold married Olaf's sister Edith, the daughter of Kathinka and Hans Hansen of Port Neville. They were married aboard the Columbia Coast Mission boat *Columbia*, with Canon Greene officiating at the service. Harold and Edith had their own float camp, which they towed around the coast just as Harold's father had. Edith, an amateur historian, has written a number of articles about life on the coast and her own life in logging camps.

Edith and Harold Bendickson spent thirty-eight years living on floating camps in mainland inlets and islands on the coast north of Hardwicke Island. Moving camp is a major undertaking, as illustrated by a move they made in the 1940s from Wellbore Channel to their next logging claim at Stimpson Reef in the Johnstone Strait. The tug *Queen* stood by and waited until the steam donkey had pulled all the camp buildings, machinery and homes aboard the floats. At five in the afternoon, when the tide was ebbing, the caravan set out—the floats with the steam donkeys and other equipment, bunk-houses, and several family homes, with the Bendicksons' gas boat trailing astern. As night closed in, fog settled in around them. Radar was not used as a navigation aid on the coast in those days, and in order to avoid running aground, the skipper of the *Queen* stayed near the middle of the channel. However, other shipping was travelling along the same lane, and the occupants of the floating camp spent a tense night listening to the husky tones of the foghorns from large ships passing too close for comfort. Even more frightening, this was before the time of CBs or VHF radiophones and there was no way to contact the skipper of the *Queen*.

Edith was exhausted. She eventually went

to bed around one o'clock a.m., only to be awakened a short time later by the shouts of Harold and his brother Jim. Everyone scrambled out of their houses and watched as the huge bow of a freighter bore down on them. Miraculously, they were seen at the last moment and the ship swerved away as the huge waves in its wake washed over the floats.

When dawn came, the fog still hung low on the water, with a glimmer of sunlight shining through. Harold could tell from the position of the sun that they were too far north. He took Jim and a compass in the gas boat and went off to try to establish their position. They discovered they were twelve miles north of their destination. They reported this to the skipper of the tug and later that day they finally secured the floats at Stimpson Reef.

The Bendicksons logged Stimpson Reef for six months, then moved to Boughy Bay, also on the mainland. A year later they moved their camp north to Village Island where they stayed for several years logging in a number of different locations. They started a floating school on the camp in 1948. "Most of us were newly married with young children. We put high fences around our floats to have safe play yards."

Edith and Harold's three children, Barbara, Victor and Lorne, were born while they lived on their floating camp. When Barbara was three years old, she was rushed to the Alert Bay hospital some fifteen miles away to have her appendix out. It was a very anxious time for her parents, as she was very ill and their gas boat only made eight knots. She got there in time, and luckily the doctor was not out on another call.

Harold and Edith have kept a home on Hardwicke Island since they were married, on the land the senior Bendicksons originally settled. In June 1990, they celebrated their fiftieth wedding anniversary. There are now ten third-generation Bendicksons, many of whom are actively involved in forestry and logging, carrying on in their grandfather's footsteps.

15. Kelsey Bay • Sayward • Hkusam

On the windswept coast near Kelsey Bay are the ruins of the ancient Indian village of Xusam or Hkusam. This village, built near the southern entrance to the Salmon River, had a superb view of the Johnstone Strait and approaching Haida warriors in their battle canoes.

When the first white settlers moved to the Salmon River, Hkusam belonged to the Hahamatses tribe, part of the Kwakiutl nation. For spiritual reasons, the Hahamatses later changed their name to the Walatsuma. Their village was well located near a sandy beach for landing canoes. At their doorstep was a large, stream-fed tidal pool through which salmon passed on their way to spawn. The forest was their backyard, where giant cedars grew and were sometimes used for building canoes. The forest also provided a home for deer and other animals. Beyond the forest, mountains rose abruptly from the valley floor.

Among the lofty peaks was the mist-shrouded Hkusam Mountain, called by the Walatsumas *Hiyatsee Saklekum* ("Where the breath of the sea lions gathers at the blowhole"). They believed that a tunnel led from the ocean to the summit of the mountain and that it was the breath of the sea lions coming out of it that caused the mist.

Johnny Moon was the village chief in the late nineteenth century. His totem stood at the entrance to the village. The pole, which had been in the Moon family for more than one hundred years, was unusual as the central figure represented a white sailor dressed in uniform with gold braid, referred to by the name of Matthew Hill. The pole was Johnny Moon's "keysoo"—a great possession acquired by a chief from his ancestors. Matthew Hill's real identity has been lost over the years, but at family feasts or celebrations his legend was re-enacted by members of the tribe.

For years the Walatsumas lived in harmony with nature, sharing the salmon with the bears, eagles and gulls, and cutting only the trees that were needed for their houses or canoes. Their lives changed, however, when European traders began to bring guns, liquor and other goods. One of the traders gave Johnny Moon's son Harry a pig. The Walatsumas were not accustomed to domestic animals and believed such an animal added greatly to the prestige of its owner. When Harry was given the pig, the entire band shared in his pride.

The pig became the band's mascot and a very privileged animal indeed. A log enclosure was built to keep it safe and to prevent it from leaving the village. The children delighted in its grunting noises when they fed it fish and berries. When the little pig got big, it

The Ruby House, still standing at Port Hkusam, was once a gem in the wilderness, housing a store, post office, hotel and saloon.

Port Hkusam, Ruby House, 1914. On step (left to right): Mr. Peterson, owner, with Anna Kelsey on knee, and Ida Thomas, Mrs. Kelsey's sister. On railing (left to right): Ruth, Evelyn, Mom and Dad Kelsey.

Booming at Kelsey Bay in 1935, with George Sacht in the foreground. Harry Dyer is to the left of George, and Bill Fersch and Tommy Long are to his right.

broke down its barricade, providing old and young with great amusement as it strolled around the village. Harry realized that the pig would not try to escape, so he decided to let it run free. The natives noticed that, having forsaken its pen, the animal became much cleaner and happier, and they were more delighted than ever with their oinking showpiece.

The pig liked grubbing around on the beach, and one day when the tide was a long way out, it wandered along the shoreline past the bluff that sheltered the village. Sauntering around to the other side of the hill, it walked right into the path of a waiting cougar. The big predator leaped on the frightened pig, sinking its teeth into its back and raking it with its claws.

The pig let out a piercing scream, and the men of the village came running with guns and clubs. They found their mascot entangled with the cougar. The pig had sunk its teeth into the cat's neck, hanging on valiantly in spite of the punishment it was taking. Even after the men shot and killed the cougar with their guns, the pig kept its teeth buried in its attacker's neck until convinced that its enemy was dead.

The pig was badly hurt, but it recovered, much to the joy of the villagers, whose pride in its bravery knew no bounds. The pig basked in their admiration for the rest of its days.

Meanwhile, the days of the Walatsuma village were numbered. Liquor and European diseases took an enormous toll among the people. The population was already dwindling, even in the days of Johnny Moon.

In 1894, the Indian agent R.H. Pidcock responded to a complaint by local settlers that they were being threatened by the Indians of Hkusam village. He arrived with a large party, including Mike Manson, the local magistrate and provincial MLA. They found five hundred Hkusam natives engaged in a huge potlatch, a practice that had recently been forbidden. Pidcock threatened to arrest Chief Johnny Moon, but as one early account states, "the situation became so dangerous that the white men's lives were in jeopardy." Eventually, the chief's son Harry offered to go in his father's place.

This incident ended potlatching at Hkusam, and marked the beginning of unrestricted white settlement. Within twenty years, the Walatsuma village was abandoned. The longhouses and the Moon family totem pole have long ago rotted into the ground.

Theodore Peterson, a former cook on the square-rigged sailing ships, settled land near the mouth of the Salmon River in 1895. Danish by birth, Peterson married a Walatsuma woman and started a family. He was an industrious man, and shortly after arriving, he and his partner Ed Wilson built the Ruby House at

Hkusam. The rambling structure was a gem in the wilderness, housing a store, post office, hotel and saloon. Hkusam became the steamer stop for that part of the coast, and the Ruby House became the halfway house for weary travellers in small boats.

By the time Theodore Peterson moved to Hkusam and built the Ruby House, a number of other settlers already had occupied land farther up the Salmon River Valley, including George Arbishaw, Herb Townsend and Hans Otto Sacht.

Through the years, Otto Sacht became one of the most prominent people in the valley. He left his home in Germany at the age of fourteen and lived in New York before coming to British Columbia. He landed in Victoria in 1890 and found work with a shipping company on the Alaska run. Within three years, he had saved enough money to purchase half-ownership in a trading sloop, and it was while bartering with the Walatsumas at Hkusam that Sacht decided to make the valley his home. Like other pioneers, Sacht was no stranger to hard work, and within a few years he had cleared some land, planted a farm and built a house.

In 1898, Sacht left his homestead in the care of a friend and returned to Germany, where he met his wife. Together they returned to the Salmon River Valley, and they built their first trading post in 1903. The Sacht family, including seven children (six boys and one girl) was a big part of the valley's history. They were also the friends of the Walatsumas. Hans often sat with his Indian friends during their winter ceremonies; he was one of the few white people invited to the last big potlatch in 1894.

Hans Sacht lived in the valley for sixty years. In 1955, he built a new store and, for sentimental reasons, moved the big counter from the old store to the new one. The counter, which was thirty-two feet long, had been cut by the Hastings Mill Company in 1906. Since then it has been touched by the hands—and elbows—of the thousands of friends and customers who came to the Sacht store. Mr. Sacht died in 1959, at the age of 87. The store is no longer in business, but the big counter is on view at the local historical museum.

The biggest change to the valley came when the Hastings Mill Company moved in to log in 1905. Although it meant immediate prosperity for the European settlers, it caused a continuing series of environmental disasters. The company stripped the valley clean of its virgin timber, before removing its operations in 1912.

The newcomers, with little awareness of the country they had come to live in, had no idea of the disastrous effects this would have on their surroundings. Indian legends about "the

great flood" of long ago received no more credence than the story of Noah. But in February of 1918, a long cold snap with a six-inch snowfall was followed by a warm, heavy rain. A fast melt set in, and a torrent of water poured out of the frozen mountains with no forest growth to slow it. The banks of the Salmon River crumbled, dumping trees and vast amounts of debris into the flood waters. Settlers lost buildings and livestock to the rampaging waters. One resident, Hugh Jamieson, saved his cattle by climbing into the hayloft of his barn and pulling on their halter ropes to hold up their heads. When the water receded, farmers found their land covered with boulders that the flood had rolled onto the fields. Both bridges across the Salmon were washed out.

This disaster has been repeated time and again in the years since, most notably in 1975, when the Salmon River cut a new bed to the sea north of the White River junction, and again in the winter of 1990–91, when the area was declared a disaster region.

The Hastings Logging Company also made a number of changes in the administration of

Kelsey Bay Beach, 1936. Seated on log (left to right): Mrs. Kelsey, Mr. Kelsey, editor of the Victoria Times *and a local forest ranger. Standing on beach: BC Premier Duff Pattullo.*

Fisherman Fred Kohse rowing out from Kelsey Bay in 1937. Such a trip, out to Queen Charlotte Sound and back, might involve seventy or eighty miles of rowing.

Aerial view from Kelsey Bay looking over the Salmon River Valley. (George McNutt photo)

communities on the Salmon River. First, it petitioned the government for a post office, which was located at Otto Sacht's store in the valley in 1911. The post office was called Sayward, after a pioneer lumberman. The company was also instrumental in having a government wharf built at Kelsey Bay, on the northeastern side of the Salmon River. Port Hkusam offered only an anchorage for the Union steamships and other large vessels. The new facility at Kelsey Bay allowed ships to come alongside, rather than heaving-to in the channel and having the mail and freight transported to the Ruby House by small boat.

In 1925, Theodore Peterson sold the Ruby House to Mr. and Mrs. Fred Kohse Sr., who

Kelsey Bay store and post office in the 1940s.

Delivery van for Smith's Store, Kelsey Bay, driven by Les Smith, 1932.

turned the old hotel/saloon into their family home. The saloon was the living area, with a drum heater serving as a furnace. Their two sons, Fred and Gerald, were raised there. Fred Jr. described the sleeping rooms as being more like cupboards, and none too well insulated. At times during the winter, his bed had a blanket of snow covering it.

Fred Kohse Jr. became a well-known fisherman along the coast. As he remembers, "I was twelve years old when I moved to the Sayward district. When I was thirteen I began rowboat trolling in the Johnstone Strait. There was a lot of salmon in the strait and we were getting fifty cents apiece, which was a lot of money as this was during the Depression of the 1930s.

"Everyone in those days had rowboats. You either built one yourself or bought one, that was the mode of getting around. The loggers used to row from one camp to another for their jobs. With rowboat trolling we just used a single line and a spoon—that was the cheapest method of going out fishing. Starting in with rowboat trolling and starting to make a few dollars, it sort of gets into your blood, the fishing. It's sort of an adventurous life."

Mr. and Mrs. William Kelsey had lived on the coast since 1906, most of that time on Hardwicke Island. They moved across the channel in 1922 and opened a store, telegraph station and post office in the bay that was later named after them. The people of the valley objected to the area being called Kelsey Bay instead of Sayward. They posted their own sign on the dock alongside the one that said Kelsey Bay. This controversy has continued through the years, although the hostilities were softened somewhat when the three Kelsey girls married three of Otto Sacht's sons from Sayward.

In 1928, the Kelseys sold their holdings to Herbert Stanley Smith, a former lighthouse keeper who had married Annie Lewis, the daughter of early settlers who, coincidentally, had been the previous owners of the Kelsey store. The Smiths had five children, and they continued operating the store and post office

Kohse's store still stands near the Kelsey Bay waterfront.

Kelsey Bay docks in 1946. The Union Steamship Venture is tied at the dock, with fishing boats and government telegraph boat at the float.

A school bus driven by Bill Fersch, who moved from Graham Island in the Queen Charlottes and bought the Kelsey Bay store from the Smiths.

until 1941, when their second eldest daughter, Joan, and her husband, Bill Fersch, took over the business.

By 1944, the highway between Campbell River and Kelsey Bay was completed. Cars, not boats, became the main mode of transportation and life in the valley changed. Ten years later hydro came through, and in 1967, a ferry began servicing the northern part of the island. The ferry, named *Lady Rose*, ran from Kelsey Bay to Beaver Cove, Alert Bay and Sointula, and stayed overnight before returning to Kelsey Bay. It was mainly a foot-passenger service, as the vessel carried only three cars. In 1969, BC Ferries took over the run.

Right: Hilda Kohse with her great-granddaughter Margie Parsons.

Far right: Kelsey Bay/Sayward pioneers George Sacht (at left) and Fred Kohse.

Boats are crammed into the Kelsey Bay marina, taking refuge from a blow in Johnstone Strait.

BC Ferries once stopped at Kelsey Bay en route to Prince Rupert. Shown is the Queen of Prince Rupert, *which now sails from Port Hardy.*

A view of Kelsey Bay from a sailboat on Johnstone Strait.

An unusual craft, bedecked with flowers, at Kelsey Bay.

The town of Sayward was incorporated in 1968, and by 1970 its amenities included a firehall, police station, bank, liquor store and town hall, as well as the Kelsey Bay recreation centre. Although the post office is located in Sayward, Kelsey Bay is still open for business. There is a government dock with limited moorage. Mrs. H. Kohse, formerly of Hkusam, moved to Kelsey Bay in 1957 and operated the store on the dock until her death in 1989. Her old home, the Ruby House, remained in the Kohse family until it was sold in 1980. It needs repairs, but it is still standing.

16. Port Neville

Port Neville is an almost landlocked inlet that works its way fifteen miles inland through the majestic Coast Range of mountains. It lies about eight miles north of Hardwicke Island. For many years this narrow body of water has offered protection to fishing boats and other small craft running for shelter from sudden storms on Johnstone Strait.

Port Neville was named by Captain Vancouver in 1792, for Lieutenant John Neville, Royal Marines (Queen's Regiment). The mountains around Port Neville were named Nelson Range, Collingwood and Hardy in memory of British heroes at the battle of Trafalgar.

Warriors of the Kwakiutl nation once roamed these mountains and lowlands. Their main village was built on the grassy fields near the Fulmore River near the head of the inlet. The Fulmore was once a prolific salmon-spawning river, and the Indians built large houses along the banks with open, central fire-places where they smoked the salmon. All that remains of these first inhabitants are petro-glyphs on the rocks near Robbers Nob, and an extensive midden on the opposite shore. The village itself disappeared before white settlement. It is believed that marauding Haida warriors took the villagers by surprise and slaughtered them.

Port Neville holds a special place in my heart, as it is the place I was born. It was also the first Canadian home for my mother, Ferdinanda Maria Louise Hansen, and my eldest sister, Edith, who had travelled together from Norway to join my father Ingebrigt in 1925. It was a coincidence that they came to a small village where another couple named Hansen—Hans and Kathinka—had already settled. Kathinka and my mother became close friends. Their youngest daughter, named Edith, was two years older than my sister, and the two girls became lifelong friends, known as the two Edie Hansens from Port Neville.

Kathinka's husband was called "Hans the Boatman." To me, he is identified with the story of Port Neville. Hans was one of those people with determination, skill and an unfaltering faith in himself, who was able to achieve his goals in spite of the many obstacles life put in his way.

Hans was one of the early European settlers on the coast. Born in Norway in 1859, he went to sea with his father at the age of fourteen. He arrived in Gastown in 1883 aboard the schoo-

Sigurd Haga (standing), my mother Ferdinanda Hansen and my sister Edith, soon after they arrived at Port Neville, 1925.

ner *Esmeralda* and went to work for the Hastings Mill. He was making plans to book passage on a ship bound for Norway when a hunting accident changed his life. His left hand had to be amputated. This was a profound blow for the young man, thousands of miles away from home in the raw pioneering country of Canada's west coast. Fortunately, once the stump healed he was able to commission a blacksmith to make an iron hook that could be strapped to his arm. The iron hook was fitted with a square hole into which the end of an oar could be put. This allowed him more use of the arm and enabled him to row a boat.

For the next few years Hans held a number of jobs, including one as part-time postmaster at George Black's hotel and store in Gastown. It was Hans Hansen who rowed down Burrard Inlet to meet the first coast-to-coast train that pulled into Port Moody on July 4, 1886. After receiving the mail, he rowed it back to George Black's hotel.

Hans continued to work in and around Vancouver for the next few years, but he grew restless, and in the spring of 1889, at the age of

The Hans Hansen family (left to right): Edith (Edie), Arthur (Art), Lillian (Lily), Olaf (Ole), Karen and Billy Hansen, 1929.

thirty, he outfitted a rowing sloop and headed north along the coast. As he rowed north, he traded with the Indians and looked for land. In Bickley Bay, next to the boom town of Shoal Bay on East Thurlow Island, he met another Norwegian settler by the name of Nels Hiorth. The two men remained in Bickley Bay for a couple of years, running a store for the camps operating there.

When Nels went back to Vancouver, Hans also moved on. Continuing north along the coast, he came to Port Neville in the spring of 1891 and decided to settle in the small bay on the southern shore near the entrance to the inlet.

Hansen spent the next few years clearing and fencing land, building a home, and constructing huts for travellers or people stopping

Boat day at Port Neville. At centre is Mrs. Katrinka Hansen with her dog.

to pick up mail or freight when the Union Steamship boats arrived. He charged twenty-five cents a night for cabins, plus twenty-five cents for meals. Many could not pay, and others would leave tobacco, ground coffee or other useful items.

On November 1, 1895, Hans Hansen was sworn in as the postmaster at Port Neville, and the Union steamships began to bring in the mail on a regular schedule. Like many places along the coast at that time, Port Neville had no landing or wharf for large vessels. The Union vessels had a special door off the cargo deck just above the water, and small boats came alongside to unload and take on freight or mail, while the ship lay at anchor or was hove-to in the channel.

Hans kept a diary in 1895, and his daughter Edith (now Bendickson) preserved it. According to Edith, her father's postal district covered a large area, from Knight Inlet in the north to Loughborough Inlet in the south. People rowed or sailed to the post office as there were very few boats with motors in those days.

After logging some of the virgin timber on his land, Hans cleared and fenced an area where fruit trees and a garden were planted. He kept cows and chickens, and before long was shipping produce to Harry Fillon's store in Vancouver, as well as Pope's store and hotel at Port Harvey. His jobs were many and varied. He helped settle disputes in the Indian village, shipped fur for the trappers, helped loggers with their booming, hand-logged, and even tried mining.

The Matilpi Indian reservation was at the head of Port Neville Inlet when Hans the boatman arrived. The Indians lived there for many years after the turn of the century, and Edith Bendickson remembers her father and Chief Matilpi smoking their pipes and talking about

old times. Hans had learned to speak the Indian dialect. "This really pleased Matilpi Sam, who would grin mischievously at us children, knowing we couldn't understand a word they were saying!"

In 1897, Hans Hansen married Elizabeth, an English widow with a two-year-old son. But Elizabeth became seriously ill a year after the marriage, and she died at Shoal Bay. Her young son Willy was left in the care of his stepfather, who continued living at Port Neville, working and caring for the young boy.

As the new century came in, Hans went back to Norway for a visit. Sam Givens, a close friend, looked after the homestead and Willy during that time. In 1903, Hans returned to Port Neville with a new bride, Kathinka, a beautiful young woman who had taught school in Tonsberg, his home town in Norway. The next year, Sam Givens became the caretaker once again while Kathinka and Hans travelled by sloop to Vancouver. There she gave birth to their eldest daughter, Karen, at St. Luke's Home, the first Anglican hospital in the city. When the mother and child were strong enough, they returned to Port Neville.

Five years later, the Hansen family moved to New Westminster so that Willy, then called Billy, and their daughter Karen could go to school. They lived there for the next seven years. During that time Hans worked as circulation manager for the *World* newspaper. When the *World* went into receivership just before World War I, Hans went gillnetting on the Fraser River. With only one hand he could not pull in the net, so Kathinka went out in the boat with him.

The Hansens' son and daughter, Olaf and Lily, were born in New Westminster in 1909 and 1912 respectively. Arthur and Edith Hansen were born in 1916 and 1918, after the family had returned to Port Neville. By this time

Kathinka was ailing much of the time. Karen, who was fourteen, had to take care of the family.

Hansen began building a two-storey log house back in 1920. You can still see it at Port Neville today. Building the house was difficult for Hans because of his disability: his friends came by to help when he had to lift the logs in place by hand-winch or block-and-tackle. The house was completed in 1924, and the following year, the office of postmaster came back to the Hansen family. Karen was sworn in as postmistress, a position she held until her retirement in 1960.

In 1925, Karen opened a big store that supplied that part of the coast for many years. The

Above left: An old man known only as "Six-Shooter Brown" kept his boat in the slough on the Hans Hansen homestead at Port Neville. He carried a pistol in his belt and made it clear he would use it if necessary.

Above right: A foresty vessel leaving Port Neville Inlet.

From left: my sister Edith, Alice Larson, Karen Hansen, the postmistress and storekeeper at Port Neville, and Mrs. Gus Erickson from Hardwicke Island.

The government dock and log home built by Hans Hansen in 1925.

government wharf was built in 1928, and steamships could come alongside to load and unload freight. That same year, the Hansens became the agents for Standard Oil, and vessels could pick up fuel at the government dock.

My parents' home in Port Neville Inlet was destroyed by a raging forest fire a few months after my mother and sister Edith arrived there. Other homes were also destroyed. My parents lost everything in that fire, including all my mother's personal possessions, such as her guitar and the family photos she had brought from Norway. They were fortunate that the Hans Hansen family was able to take them in until they got re-established.

My family continued living at Port Neville for the next few years. My sister Louise and I were born aboard the Mission ship *Columbia* during that time. After we moved away, Hans and Kathinka stayed on in Port Neville, and their daughters and sons married into other coastal families. Olaf married Lilly Bendickson, the only daughter of Hans and Gertrude Bendickson of Hardwicke Island. Olaf and Lilly have lived at Port Neville since their marriage in 1937 and continue to live a self-sufficient life. The post office was still open in the summer of 1991, and Olaf and Lilly's daughter Lorna was the postmistress, continuing a tradition that goes all the way back to

1895. Their post office uses the same implements and cancellation stamp that were in use before the turn of the century.

The big store and fuel docks are only a memory now, but Port Neville still offers a safe anchorage, and when the weather gets rough in Johnstone Strait, the harbour is full of small craft, just as it was a century ago.

The Hans Hansen homestead and the docks where the boats moor and the Union Steamship vessels used to stop. (George McNutt photo)

17. Minstrel Island

Minstrel Island, like nearby Bones Bay, Negro Rock and Sambo Point, is believed to have been named because of a talented troupe of amateur actors on the HMS *Amethyst*, which was taking Lord Dufferin, then Governor General of Canada, to visit the Indian village of Metlakatla on the north coast in 1876. The amateur actors among the crew performed black-face minstrel shows that captivated audiences at the settlements where the *Amethyst* stopped, and resulted in this scattering of names in the Minstrel Island area.

The island lies near the mouth of Knight Inlet amid some of the most spectacular scenery in the world. In the distance, beyond the head of Knight Inlet, are glacier-clad peaks as far as the eye can see. Among them is the lofty Mt. Waddington, British Columbia's highest mountain, embracing the clouds almost 14,000 feet above sea level.

In centuries past, the coast around Minstrel Island was Kwakiutl country. The area is rich in Indian history and has produced artifacts dating back thousands of years. When white men came, they took the land and placed the Indians on reserves. Native villages in the area have now vanished. Even the Mamalilaculla reserve on Village Island, once one of the largest on the coast, has been abandoned. It was the people of Mamalilaculla who hosted the "Christmas Tree Potlatch," the last big potlatch ever held on the coast.

The first non-native settlers on Minstrel Island were Oscar Soderman and his wife, Sydney, who arrived in 1905 and built their homestead where the main village is today. Like other hand-loggers, Oscar preferred stands of timber near the water, where he could fall trees directly into the salt-chuck rather than haul them out by winch or oxen. The area around Minstrel was rich in timber, with giant Douglas firs growing on the rocky peninsulas. There were about sixty logging outfits working around Minstrel when Soderman moved there, with one-man operations in almost every bay and several bigger outfits as well.

With the demand for supplies growing, the Union Steamship Company made Minstrel Island one of its scheduled stops. By 1907, Tom Bennet and John Armstrong had opened a small general store which carried food staples and gear for working in the woods. The store was called Armstrong and Bennet. Tom Bennet was one of those people who could turn his hand to almost anything; at times he served as a lawyer, mechanic, and in an emergency even a medical doctor.

The Minstrel Island Hotel was also built in 1907, by Neil Hood, an entrepreneur who saw there was money to be made in the hotel business. Among other things, the hotel became a recruiting centre for loggers. With the Union steamship stopping every two weeks, it gave the men the opportunity to stay over and look for a job at one of the camps. If there was nothing available they could ship out again on the *Cassiar*'s return trip.

There was a saloon at the hotel that stacked up a reputation as one of the toughest places on the coast. Weekends were wild, with men coming in from all the outlying camps. If the

Life at Minstrel, around 1914.

A smorgasbord picnic at Minstrel Island in the 1920s. Note the semi-formal dress.

Minstrel Islanders get together on their float houses, 1935.

Cassiar was expected, there might be as many as 500 people milling around looking for something to do. Many of the men ended up in the bar. The drinkers at the Minstrel Island Hotel got a reputation for consuming more beer than in any other licensed lounge in British Columbia.

Logging remained the main industry around Minstrel Island for many years, and drinking beer wasn't the only social activity. "Boat Day" and the Saturday night dances were what people looked forward to the most. Minstrel Island was one of the places that booked the Rhythm Busters, the touring band from Heriot Bay, to play at the dances. People arrived from as far south as Hardwicke Island and Kelsey Bay and as far north as Port Hardy.

The Canadian Fishing Company cannery at nearby Bones Bay on East Cracroft Island, built in 1920, also had many employees during the summer months when the fish were running. Jack Dorman was the plant manger at Bones Bay for many years.

Between the logging and fishing industries, boatbuilders, mechanics and machinists were always in demand. During the summer months, when logging and fishing were in full swing, they were kept working around the clock. If a fish-packer or seiner broke down at the height of the salmon run, thousands of dollars could be lost. During the winter months, tradesmen were needed at the logging camps, which operated throughout the year except during fire season and very cold winters with lots of snow.

Clarence and Nellie Cabeen settled on Minstrel Island in the 1920s. Clarence, a first-class machinist, opened a machine shop on the island which served that part of the coast for the next twenty years.

The same year, the George Wilson family moved to the island. George, who ran a successful logging operation in the area, was

nicknamed "Bull Moose." The couple were known as Ma and Pa Wilson.

Roy and Georgie Halliday from Kingcome Inlet built a new store on Minstrel in 1935. They sold it in 1940 to Ben and June Reid, and it changed hands again in 1944 when it was sold to Lawrence Rose. Roy, who was trained

Betsy, John, Francis and Robert MacDonald on their floating home at Minstrel Island, 1940s.

Minstrel Island from the sea, with the hotel in the background.

Below left: Aerial view of Minstrel Island Resort, as it is today. (photo courtesy of Grant and Sylvia Douglas)

Below right: Dogs travelling on boats can be a nuisance if they are left unattended dockside. Minstrel Island has its own rules posted on the wharf: "Dogs not on leash will be cheerfully shot."

as a mechanic and had a gift for working with wood, built a marine ways and boat-repair shop on the island. People from many parts of the coast relied on the boatyard. The yard closed in the early 1960s, and people say the island has never been quite the same.

In 1922, Neil Flood bought the Port Harvey Hotel, winched it onto a float and towed it down to Minstrel Island, where it was winched back on land. The main floor was used as a community hall and the rooms upstairs were rented out. The "Hall," as the islanders called it, was used for dances, Christmas and community functions. The building also housed the first post office on the island.

Among the best-known people along this part of the coast are Merle Hadley and his wife, Edith, who settled in the 1930s on the mainland near the entrance to Call Inlet. Their two children, Bill and Sid, were born while they were living there. The boys attended school at Minstrel. One morning, while chugging to school in their small boat powered by a four-horsepower Easthope, the boat suddenly stopped moving. They were even more surprised when the boat and the object with which it had collided began rising out of the water. They were getting a lift on the back of a whale! Within minutes, the whale submerged and the boys continued on their way. They never told anyone their whale of a story. After

all, who would believe them? However, the Adderly family, who lived near the pass, saw what happened and told the story on their next visit to the village.

The Hadley homestead on Chatham Channel is now called Hadley Bay. Bill Hadley was killed in an accident at Hadley Bay on November 24, 1981, at the age of forty-four. He accomplished a lot during his lifetime. He was survived by his wife, Ruth; their three children, Lynne, Dale and Rod; his parents; and his brother, Sid. Logging entrepreneur Harold Bendickson said, "Logging on the coast will never be the same without Bill!" Another friend remembered Bill in these words: "He was loved by his family, liked by his friends and needed by everyone on the coast."

While the Hadley boys were growing up, they helped their father in the mill at Hadley Bay. Bill was interested in machinery and learned to improvise by watching and helping Clarence Cabeen in his shop at Minstrel. In 1966, Bill opened his own machine shop in Hadley Bay. He was a first-class machinist who repaired logging equipment and marine engines. Boats were towed to his shop from as far away as Prince Rupert to be repaired.

In 1976, Bill started a freight-barge business, called Hadley Bay Marine Company Ltd. The barge was the former Denman Island ferry, *Catherine Graham*, a scow-like ship measuring 120 by 34 feet. She was built in 1953 by Fauchon Engineering Works Ltd. in Campbell River, and was equipped with landing ramps, ideal for loading heavy machinery. The *Catherine Graham* was altered and relaunched in April 1981, as the *Sea Roamer*, named after another vessel the Hadleys had owned.

Mr. and Mrs. Hugh Herbison opened the first boarding school on Minstrel Island in 1944, making schooling available to local children as well as those who were too far away to commute and who would otherwise have had to rely on correspondence courses. Mr. Herbison was trained as a minister and his wife as a music teacher.

The Hadley mill was destroyed by fire in 1989. In September 1991, Merle and Edith sold Hadley Bay and moved to Kelsey Bay. The new owners were Bing and Eleanor Jagger.

By the end of the 1950s, life around Minstrel Island had slowed down. The Canadian Fishing Company cannery at Bones Bay had closed its doors in 1949. The Union Steamship Company no longer served the coast, and the small logging outfits were being taken over by timber giants like Crown Zellerbach.

The hotel, which continued to operate, changed hands a number of times. Neil Hood and Alan MacDonald were the owners between 1930 and 1963. It was while Alan MacDonald had the hotel up for sale, that the late

Above: The Blow Hole was named after the strong gusts of wind that funnelled down the eastern side of the island.

Left: At Minstrel Island, now a popular vacation destination, there is little evidence of its stormy past.

Bones Bay cannery and workers' village on West Cracroft Island was owned by the Canadian Fishing Company. It was one of the large cannery operations on the coast in the 1930s and 1940s. Many of the people who worked at Bones Bay spent their leisure time at Minstrel, only a three-mile boat ride away.

Right: A picnic on Minstrel Island, 1920s.

Below: Mrs. Ida Wilson of Minstrel, with her goats.

Pearlie Sherdahl dropped by for a drink. He was less than sober, and the manager refused to serve him and asked him to leave the premises. Sherdahl, a logging entrepreneur, became so angry he caught the first plane to Vancouver in the morning. There he bought the Minstrel Island Hotel, and then returned to fire the manager. The Sherdahls were very much part of island community until 1980, when Pearlie's skiff overturned in Knight Inlet and he was drowned.

Ed and Margid Carter purchased the remainder of the resort in 1973, including the store, 118 acres of land and a diesel generator that supplied power for the settlement. Ed was a capable but gruff individual, liked by some and disliked by many. He got himself into trouble on Minstrel and as the story goes,

rather than appear in court he just disappeared. He left Minstrel on a Friday morning during the second week of November 1981, on a float plane on which he'd installed extra tanks for long-distance flying. He had a noon appointment at Kingcome Inlet and a one o'clock meeting at Port McNeill. His court case was the following Monday.

At precisely twelve noon, his plane was spotted through the clouds over Kingcome. It appeared again about ten minutes later, heading out through the cut toward Sullivan Bay. That was the last time anyone saw Ed Carter.

An air-sea and land search was launched; it became one of the most expensive searches in the province's history. A friend of the family hired a helicopter and even brought in a well-known psychic from Vancouver, who had located other aircraft that had gone missing. But not this time, even though Ed Carter was known as a very capable flier and, according to his wife, "to crash in an aircraft wasn't Ed's style."

Minstrel Island has had a stormy past, but it remains one of the special places along the coast. Grant and Sylvia Douglas bought the Minstrel Island resort in 1989 and had a grand opening of the new facilities on the July first weekend in 1991. The new floats have a fuel barge and room for quite a number of boats. The fishing is good, and there are many delightful walks around the island. Or you can just lie back in your deck chair and enjoy the wonderful scenery.

Left: Bill and Ruth Hadley at Hadley Bay, 1973.

Below: The Sea Roamer on the ways at Hadley Bay, 1979.

18. Kingcome Inlet

The Halliday Farm lies at the head of Kingcome Inlet, where the Kingcome River winds its way down the mountain into a silt-green sea. On the river's western banks, nestled against a forest of cedar, alder and hemlock, are the farm buildings. They are surrounded by the long, sweeping, silver-gold grass of the delta, and are cradled by the sheer cliffs and glacial peaks of the Kingcome Range. It is an artist's paradise and the setting of Margaret Craven's famous novel *I Heard the Owl Call My Name.*

The inlet lies more than 300 miles north of Vancouver. For almost a century, the head of the spectacular fjord has been home to four generations of the Halliday family. In 1894, Ernest Halliday Sr., his brother William and his brother-in-law Harry Kirkham, rowed from Comox in a small open sloop fitted with oars. They wanted to look at the wild meadows at the head of Kingcome Inlet with the idea of using them as a site to graze cattle. They found a broad, open plain and a rich river delta abounding with eulachon and trout. The land far surpassed their expectations. They decided to make it their home and immediately went to work building a log cabin.

When the cabin was finished, the three men returned to Comox to get supplies and to escort Ernest's wife, Elizabeth, and their two children, Reginald and Dorothy, to their wilderness home. They negotiated for passage aboard the steamer *Coquitlam*, heading north on April 15, 1895. A few days later the settlers, livestock and supplies were put ashore on the Kingcome River delta. For the remainder of that day and into the dusky evening they packed their possessions piece by piece to their cabin a mile upstream. When it grew dark, what remained to be moved was left for the following day. During the night, an exceptionally high spring tide floated much of the gear out to sea; other goods were left sodden on the beach. Luckily, the livestock was tethered on higher ground. It was a hard beginning for the newcomers, but like other pioneers along the coast, they had a great deal of determination and made the most of what was left.

Two years after their arrival, when their third child was expected, Ernest and Elizabeth and their two sons rowed back to Comox. It was the middle of winter and bitterly cold. The trip was anything but pleasant: high winds lashed Johnstone Strait, and blinding snowstorms made progress even more difficult. Three weeks later, they arrived in Comox, where William was born, and when mother and son were strong enough the family rowed back to their wilderness home.

The Hallidays had seven children in all. Two died at birth; the others were delivered at the homestead. William died at eighteen from tuberculosis, but the rest of the children have

Below left: Gwayner Reserve, three miles up Kingcome River, is seldom visited. (Jim Spilsbury photo, c. 1965)

Below right: The totem of Chief Johnny Scow of the Tsawawdain-euk tribe of the Kwakiutl, on the Gwayner Reserve up the Kingcome River.

enjoyed long, happy lives.

When Ernest and Elizabeth arrived back in Kingcome with William, other settlers were moving in. Besides William Halliday and Harry Kirkham, there were the Smith brothers, the Landsdowne family, and a bachelor by the name of Harry Kirby. Kirby, originally from England, came to Kingcome Inlet at the age of nineteen and stayed for the rest of his life. A quiet man with many friends, he loved gardening and reading. Whenever he had new guests, they were given a sharply cut diamond

Aerial view of Kingcome Inlet. (photo copyright Tim Poole)

Kingcome Inlet. (photo copyright Tim Poole)

The Halliday family in front of their first homestead.

and asked to write their name on one of the window panes.

The families worked hard. They planted orchards and gardens; they smoked fish and venison. The rich soil was ideal for growing crops. They were aided by their neighbours, the Tsawawdain-euk Indians, part of the Kwakiutl nation, who centuries before had built a village upstream from where the newcomers settled. Their pictographs once adorned the giant cliff walls of Kingcome, and their tall totem welcomed visitors at the mouth of the river. Now both pictographs and totem have vanished with weather and time.

From the Indians the newcomers learned the native way of fishing, hunting, trapping, and smoking fish and game. They learned how to navigate the swift-running currents of the river in a dugout canoe and how to survive in the wilderness. In turn, the settlers offered comfort when a tribe member was sick or dying, and served as the Indians' contact with a more modern world. Together the two cultures co-existed, sharing the same river and the same land.

However, after Ernest's brother, William, became Indian agent for much of the coast in 1906, mistrust began to replace harmony. William was responsible for enforcing the federal law banning the potlatch, which caused much bitterness among the Indians.

The homesteaders of Kingcome became fairly self-sufficient. Christmas shopping was done by catalogue, and staples were rowed in from Alert Bay. Ernest made the dawn-to-dusk trip to Alert once a month for seventeen years.

The Halliday farm as it looks today.

There he sold beef and butter for ten cents a pound, and brought back flour, sugar, tea or coffee with the money in hand. There was never anything left over. His beef and butter account did not show a profit until 1912.

This profit marked the beginning of a new era in the inlet. Industry began to move in. The Powell River Company had set up a logging operation at the head of the inlet, and the Stump Cannery was in full operation at Charles Creek. Union Steamship vessels were now making regular calls, and new families were in with enough children to open a school. There was a ready market for butter, vegetables, beef and fruit, which meant the homesteaders could sell all they could produce.

Miss Frances Bradish was one of the inlet's first schoolteachers and Reg Halliday was one of her first pupils. By then he was nineteen, older than the other students but obviously the teacher's favourite. When Miss Bradish returned to her home in Ontario after the term was over, she corresponded with Reg and four years later, in 1918, she returned to Kingcome Inlet and married him. The young couple took land adjacent to the family farm, and together the two families worked the land.

The end of 1918 also saw the completion of a two-storey house that Ernest Sr. and Elizabeth had built alongside their old log cabin. It still stands today as a spacious and dignified piece of architecture that blends well with its surroundings. Both houses are bordered by brilliant gardens, where giant sunflowers stand nine feet tall. A large verandah opens on a hallway and a cozy living room with easy chairs, sofas and low coffee tables covered with magazines. The glow from kerosene lamps flickers along walls of leather-bound books, old silver and delicate china—although there is electricity if anyone wants to use it.

In the old days, the door to the Halliday home was never locked, and the table was always set for company. For their generous ways, the Hallidays were known as Mr. and Mrs. Hospitality, and when the old folks passed on, Reg and Frances inherited the title because they too were kind, generous people.

A number of settlers came and went from the inlet. Of the Hallidays, only Reg lived there his entire life. He was six months old when he arrived at Kingcome in 1895, and eighty-one when he was forced to leave because of illness. According to his brother Ernest, he loved the valley deeply and was loved by all who knew him. He looked upon his lifetime in the Kingcome Valley as an era of prosperity, and, although he began regular chores on the farm when he was only five years old, he was never heard to complain. He never was drunk, never drove a car, and never said a bad word about anyone. He smoked two cigarettes daily. Reg and Frances' son, Allen, is now

The Halliday family home, built in 1917–18.

looking after the farm at Kingcome. The land has been sold, and the original homestead now belongs to the Ducks Unlimited organization.

Kingcome Inlet is off the beaten track for most visitors, but the fortunate few who venture that far north return year after year to enjoy the good fishing and the spectacular mountain scenery. Like most of the inlets of the upper coast, Kingcome's depths are considerable and anchorages are few. The Admiralty charts show that all of the inlet is more than forty fathoms deep right up to the river delta. The only place with reasonable depth is Anchorage Cove. From there, visitors travel by dinghy for a visit to the old Halliday Farm.

Roy and Georgie Halliday's house at Moore Bay.

19. Sullivan Bay

Sullivan Bay, about 280 miles north of Vancouver, lies on the north side of North Broughton Island. It was one of the main fuel stops on the coast for float and biplane traffic between 1945 and the late 1950s. It was also a key centre for fishermen, loggers and settlers from the outer islands and isolated inlets.

Located near the junction of Sutlej Channel and Wells Passage, Sullivan Bay is right next door to the open Pacific Ocean rolling in through Queen Charlotte Sound. In the summer months, the area around Sullivan Bay is a wilderness paradise, with a network of islands interlaced by channels and swift-running currents. These same surroundings can be bleak and cold during the winter when the winds sweep down off the high Coast Mountains and fog rolls in from Queen Charlotte Sound.

North Broughton and other islands around Queen Charlotte Sound were Kwakiutl country for centuries. Occasionally a shipwrecked sailor or a weary oarsman rowing the coast sought shelter on the island's north shore. Sometimes these men stayed on, married Indian women and joined the village.

The weather and remoteness of North Broughton discouraged settlement. Not until the early part of this century, when fish canneries and logging camps opened on a large scale and the Union steamships were making regular calls, did Europeans begin arriving.

Among the first settlers were George and Estelle Thompson. Estelle had crossed Canada on a stagecoach. After arriving in Vancouver in 1902, she travelled to Shoal Bay on East Thurlow Island by Union steamship, where she met George Thompson, a logger. They were married and moved to North Broughton. George and Estelle lived and logged on the British Columbia coast around Simoom Sound and the Broughton Islands for the next sixteen years. During that time, they had four children. Myrtle, their second, was born in Vancouver in 1916. She was three weeks old when

Aerial view of Sullivan Bay shows how North Broughton Island shelters it from strong winds, making it an ideal anchorage. (George McNutt photo)

Left: A view along the floats of the Sullivan Bay resort.

Below: Main Street, Sullivan Bay, Fire Department No. 1.

Bottom: Market Street, Sullivan Bay.

she moved to Simoom Sound in her mother's arms.

When the Thompson children reached school age, they went to Vancouver or New Westminster to attend school, but they always went home for their summer vacations. When Myrtle was ten years old, the Thompson family moved to Vancouver, but she never forgot the wilderness country of her childhood and vowed to return. Twenty-five years later, her wish came true. By then she was married to Bruce Collinson, a motorcycle buff from Kelowna, and they had two children.

"It was a twist of fate," Myrtle recalled. "I never thought Bruce would leave his bikes, but he developed double pneumonia in 1944 and his doctor recommended we move to the country where the air was fresh. I phoned my old friend Louis Mackay at Echo Bay and within a few weeks we were back in the country I had yearned for."

During their stay in Echo Bay on Baker Passage, Myrtle and Bruce took a trip over to Kinnaird Island, where a number of buildings on floats were for sale. They liked the setup. With the idea of starting an aircraft refuelling depot, they purchased the float houses from Fred Peterson and had them towed to Sullivan Bay, where there was better protection from the weather. An inspector from the Department of Transport later told them it was one of the best float plane harbours he had seen.

There were no other settlers in Sullivan Bay when the Collinsons arrived with their village. All traces of a Japanese logging camp that had been there years earlier had vanished. But the village soon came alive. The post office, which had been closed for more than a year, was reopened. The Collinsons had marine fuel, some supplies, and a coffeepot for visitors.

As the sign on the float house indicates, the Collinsons' floating village was towed to Sullivan Bay from O'Brian Bay on Kinnaird Island.

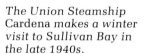

One of their first visitors was Jim Spilsbury, who arrived in his Waco Standard, a four-place biplane. "I'll never forget that day," Myrtle says. "It was the first time we met Jim. He

was selling and servicing radiotelephones, and we bought one, then sat down with him and talked about more serious business."

"You know," said Jim, "I'm going to start an airline to service the coast."

"That's great news!" said Myrtle. "I'll work for you."

Within a year, Jim had incorporated Queen Charlotte Airlines, and after a tough battle with Canadian Pacific Airlines, his company was eventually servicing most of the coast south of Prince Rupert. QCA soon became the third largest airline in Canada, with more than twenty aircraft and several hundred employees.

Sullivan Bay was the refuelling station for QCA planes on their northern run. The man who made this possible was Ernie Carswell of Standard Oil, who arranged for the tanks and floats to be installed and the aircraft fuel to be delivered. When the installation was complete, the Collinsons had 8,000 gallons of 105 octane and 1,000 gallons of 80 octane fuel for smaller aircraft. As well, they had 6,500 gallons of marine fuel, of which 1,500 gallons was diesel.

About twenty fish boats were among the Collinsons' regular customers. The logging camps picked up their fuel in thousand-gallon tanks. The Collinsons supplied the tanks, and at one time there were hundreds out on location. Myrtle recalls the days during the first stage of the operation before they had Esso aircraft fuel. Jim Spilsbury had dropped in and was filling up the tanks of his aircraft. "I could see he was laughing and when I questioned

The Union Steamship Cardena makes a winter visit to Sullivan Bay in the late 1940s.

A rare photo of two Stranraer Supermarine flying boats refuelling together at Sullivan Bay. Built by Vickers in Montreal, the "Strannies" were the mainstay of Queen Charlotte Airlines, once the major cargo-passenger carrier on the coast. CF-BXO is the only Stranraer still in existence.

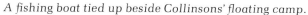

A fishing boat tied up beside Collinsons' floating camp.

Not all float plane landings are smooth. After nosing in too sharply, this plane has to be towed into the floating seaplane harbour at Sullivan Bay by a fishing boat.

him he pointed out: 'Here I am filling up with Shell oil, at a Standard Oil dealer, beneath a Home Oil sign!'" The Collinsons' fuel contract was with Standard Oil. Home Oil had been the original supplier when the village belonged to Fred Peterson, and the sign had not yet been changed.

Besides being a refuelling depot, J.B. Collinson's was a fish camp, cafe, laundry, post office and general store, and it had over-night accommodation for twenty-eight people. As well, the Union Steamship vessels were calling every couple of weeks, alternating Allison Harbour with Sullivan Bay. During the summer months, when there was constant air traffic, Bruce and Myrtle seldom saw each other except over an evening meal. In their

peak year, 1954, the Collinsons had 3,000 landings.

On a typical day, Bruce would be out servicing the planes and Myrtle would be looking after the customers and the radiotelephone. She began each day by monitoring the weather, giving a forecast, and then calling into the logging camps to see who needed an airlift. "I loved every minute of it, and many of the people we met then are still our close friends today."

Then, changes came to the area. In 1955, Jim Spilsbury sold Queen Charlotte Airlines to a group of businessmen who renamed it Pacific Western. Within a couple of years, PWA had converted its planes from pontoons to wheels and were landing at Port Hardy. In

Inside the Collinsons' cafe at Sullivan Bay.

A small QCA float plane, the Nimpkish Queen, prepares for takeoff at Sullivan Bay.

addition, forestry practices were changing, and small logging operations were either closing down or being taken over by the giant corporations.

In 1957, the Collinsons sold out to Myrtle's uncle, Pat Germain, who ran the operation until 1971, when he sold it to Irchell Fox. Fox converted the floating village into a resort and began catering to the tourist trade. Six years later, it was taken over by Michael and Lynn Whitehead. When Michael, a pilot, was killed in a plane crash, Lynn continued to live at Sullivan Bay and kept the operation open during the summer months. She is now remarried to Pat Finnerty, also a pilot.

The resort, renamed Sullivan Bay Resorts Ltd., was as popular as ever by the summer of 1991. Fire destroyed some buildings in 1983, but they were replaced. New floats were installed. Outside of a few added conveniences, the unique village that is very much part of British Columbia's aviation history maintains its original charm.

Collinson's refuelling depot at Sullivan Bay was always busy. Here, three aircraft await fuelling at the same time.

20. Telegraph Cove

Telegraph Cove is a small cut in the rocky terrain that forms the southern entrance to the much larger Beaver Cove. It offers good protection from most weather and over the years has sheltered many boaters escaping from the sudden storms blowing along Johnstone Strait. It lies about 300 miles north of Victoria and is one of the places to book an excursion to view the Orca whales that inhabit the nearby waters of Robson Bight and Blackfish Sound.

Less than one hundred years ago, Telegraph Cove was surrounded by virgin forest growing down to the water's edge. Few woodsmen ventured in to cut the trees until 1911, when the Dominion government was building a telegraph line to the head of Vancouver Island. J.T. Phalen, the superintendent of telegraphs, came to Alert Bay to scout out a suitable site for the northern terminal of the telegraph and asked local lumberman A.W. Wastell if he knew of a nearby sheltered harbour on Vancouver Island. Wastell was familiar with that part of the coast and, pleased to be of service, asked Phalen to join him on his small cruiser, the *Lyle Edward*, for a trip across the channel. They arrived in a small cove at the southern entrance to Beaver Cove. Phalen liked the location and asked Wastell to give it a name. Without much hesitation, he named it Telegraph Cove.

When the telegraph was complete, it linked Rock Bay, Sayward, Alert Bay, Port Hardy, Port Alice, Quatsino and Telegraph Cove, the northern terminus of the line. It was a crude kind of installation, with the line strung from tree to tree up the island. Nevertheless, messages generally got through, and it was faster than delivering them to Vancouver or Victoria by boat.

Perhaps the poorest service was to Alert Bay, because there was no money in the budget for an underwater cable. A linesman stationed at Telegraph Cove transcribed the Morse message. Then, if the weather was good, the message was conveyed by boat to Alert Bay and the recipient tracked down on foot. Unclaimed messages were simply pinned up on the bulletin board outside the Alert Bay telegraph office. (By 1919, the Alert Bay office was served by direct underwater cable.)

A few years later, Wastell, who was manager of the BC Fishing and Packing Company sawmill and box factory at Alert Bay, purchased 400 acres of standing timber at Telegraph Cove. He was logging there at the beginning of World War I, and cut spruce for the Canadian Munitions Board for use in building military aircraft. In 1922, Wastell purchased Telegraph Cove from the Royal Bank of Canada, the owners of the land, and went into the saltery business with a Japanese

Right: The work crew at the Broughton Mill at Telegraph Cove in 1938. Standing (left to right): Doug MacLean, Colin Armitage, Arnie Wasden, unidentified. Front row (left to right): James Burten and Malcolm Carmichael.

Far right: Fred Wastell and James Burten, Telegraph Cove, around 1977.

firm, dry-salting salmon for overseas markets in Japan.

They used chum salmon, plentiful and inexpensive because they were not a popular fish for canning. Wastell started a small sawmill at the cove to provide wood for shipping boxes. The business prospered for a number of years, and Wastell and his Japanese colleagues became good friends. But in 1929, the saltery became a losing operation and had to be closed. At the same time, BC Packers began to use cardboard instead of wood for packing salmon, so Wastell's sawmill in Alert Bay closed as well.

Wastell's son, Fred, who had worked with his father in the BCFP sawmill, suggested they move the operation to Telegraph Cove and

twelve families. The tight little village they built at the edge of the cove still exists.

James Burten and his wife Thelma were among the early settlers who worked for the lumber company at Telegraph Cove. "Jimmie," as he is known, was working on a fish packer with his father in the 1930s when he heard that Wastell was looking for someone to run his boats in Telegraph Cove. Jim, an engineer, navigator and all-around boat operator, decided to apply for the position. "Wastell told me he'd give me a try and let me know if I had the job. I worked there for fifty years, and he never did tell me whether or not I was hired!"

Jim met his wife, Thelma, in Telegraph

Above: Telegraph Cove marina is crowded with sports fishing boats in summer.

Left: A young angler getting his limit from a fishing float at Telegraph Cove.

A mill sign at Telegraph Cove.

carry on a lumber business there. In Telegraph Cove, they revamped the small mill to cut almost anything that was needed by industry on the coast, whether it was for mining, logging or dock work. It was a well-run, prosperous mill and supported several families and a number of single men. It was the pulse of the community for more than sixty years.

In 1929, Fred Wastell and A. MacDonald became partners in the Telegraph Cove operation. They worked through the Depression years selling lumber and firewood and giving credit at their small store in exchange for wages. At first, Fred went home to Alert Bay on weekends, but the winter storms were so bad that he decided to build at Telegraph Cove. The sawmill produced lumber to build more docks, a store, post office, a school and more houses. The little mill supported ten or

Telegraph Cove hugs its heavily wooded waterfront. The flat-roofed building (at centre) was built as a barracks by the RCAF during World War Two and later was converted into a community centre.

Cove. She had grown up on Cortes Island. She went to work for the Wastells in 1928, at first helping Mrs. Fred Wastell with her two young daughters, Beatrice and Patricia. She later became the postmistress and storekeeper in the Cove, a job she held for many years. Jim and Thelma's daughter, Lorraine, was born and raised in Telegraph Cove.

"We really loved the life in the Cove," recalls Jimmie. "I never regretted leaving my job on the fish-packer. Maybe it was the accident I had in 1938 that really turned me off the job!" At that time, Jim was working as an engineer for Bill and Edna Burl aboard the *Pasanaco*. They were heading down Johnstone Strait for Seattle, fully loaded with halibut, when they hit Earl Reef off Hardwicke Island. Jim was in the kitchen helping dry the breakfast dishes for Mrs. Burl when he heard the engine bells ringing frantically astern.

"Of course it was too late to prevent the accident. The next thing I knew I was in the water. It was March and icy cold with a low mist hanging over the water. The fast-running current was rapidly taking me away from land. If it hadn't been for two of the Bendickson boys who came looking for me in their small boat, I wouldn't be here today." Jim was taken back to the Bendickson homestead on Hardwicke, where Mrs. Bendickson Sr.

Right: The Pasanaco on Earl Reef off Hardwicke Island, 1938.

Far right: The Telegraph Cove post office and store in 1985. (Fiona MacGregor photo)

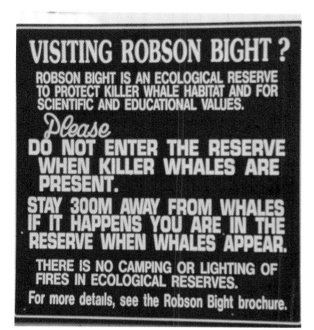

treated him for shock, virtually bringing him back to life.

There were tons of halibut free for the taking after that accident, as the bilges had to be emptied before the vessel could be refloated. Again it was the Bendickson family who worked around the clock to get the *Pasanaco* off the rocks. She went back packing fish but eventually sank off Cape Mudge.

In Telegraph Cove, Jim was in charge of the lumber company's boats, first the *Mary W*, then the *Hillicum* and finally the *Gikumi*. The company took jobs all along that part of the coast, either towing logs or hauling lumber.

During World War II, the mill at Telegraph Cove was taken over by the military, which needed lumber for the installations at Port Hardy and Coal Harbour. Instead of the dozen men who worked the operation in peacetime, there were sixty-five airmen producing lumber at a maximum rate. Some aircraft, such as the British Mosquito bomber, were still made of wood at that time, though now it was plywood.

Jim recalls an unhappy experience that took place in Telegraph Cove, soon after the outbreak of the war in the Pacific. There had been a number of Japanese people living in the Cove, most of whom were Canadians. Some worked in the mill from time to time, but most of them were fishermen or had been working in the saltery. Without warning, the military came along and took them away. They had only a short time to gather a few personal things and they had to leave behind just about everything. "We were very upset," said Jim. "They were our friends. We went into their homes and packed and stored what we could, but being on the water and them being gone for such a long time, almost everything was destroyed by dampness and mildew."

One thing the military did leave was the

mess hall, used by the air force men working the mill. It became the community hall after the war, though it is now a residence. Until 1985, the sawmill remained the main industry of Telegraph Cove. Fred Wastell passed away, in his eighties, that summer. While the mill is still there with all its original equipment, the saws are no longer working.

The sixty-foot *Gikumi*, retired from the lumber trade, now takes visitors to nearby Robson Bight to see the playground of the Orca whales, a major tourist attraction in Telegraph Cove. The province established the area as an ecological reserve in 1982 to protect the core habitat of the killer whale for research and educational purposes. Of the 300 killer whales inhabiting BC waters, more than half belong to the nineteen pods frequenting

Above left: Sign on Gikumi's berth: "Visiting Robson Bight."

Above right: The whale-watching vessel Gikumi in Robson Bight.

Marlen and Evelyn Farrant, longtime residents of Telegraph Cove, with a prize halibut at the local fishing derby.

Steps lead up from the boardwalk along the edge of the cove. (Fiona MacGregor photo)

Right: Telegraph Cove village street, 1985. (Fiona MacGregor photo)

Johnstone Strait. One aspect of their behaviour that is not yet understood is their habit of rubbing themselves on the rocky shoreline of the Bight.

Today the boardwalk village built on pilings before World War I caters to boaters, fishermen and campers who go there from all parts of the world. In the summer of 1991, there was a marina and boat ramp, a coffee shop and a small store. Telegraph Cove Resort was owned and managed by Gordie and Marilyn Graham, complete with marina, campground, and whale-watching charters run by Stubbs Island Charters.

21. Beaver Cove

Beaver Cove, with its rocky outcroppings of bluff, forms a large bite in the northeastern shoreline of Vancouver Island, about 300 miles north of Victoria. Less than a hundred years ago, Beaver Cove was a land of virgin forest. The only loggers then were the beavers that inhabited the flatlands of the Tsultan River, a tributary of the Kokish River, which empties into the waters near the head of the bay. An extensive population of beavers lived in the waters of the delta when the first settlers arrived. Some say the cove was named for these capable craftsmen, but in fact the cove was named after the Hudson's Bay Company's paddle steamer *Beaver*, which conducted a survey of the coast between 1863 and 1870.

By the turn of the century, the beaver population had all but vanished, having been hunted for their rich, water-repellent pelts. Their log dams rotted into the marshland as a new era of logging began.

The first settlers moved into Beaver Cove in the early 1900s. Captain Corney, an Englishman who had travelled north along the coast from Vancouver by small boat, was one of them. He settled near the junction of the Kokish and Tsultan rivers on land that was known as the "Old Farm." He was joined a few years later by an engineer-cum-timber cruiser by the name of Eustace Smith. Smith took a homestead just beyond Captain Corney's in the Tsultan Valley. His land was called "Smith's Clearing," and he was responsible for naming Ida and Bonanza lakes.

The first commercial venture in the area was the Beaver Cove Lumber & Pulp Company, which went into operation in 1917 under the management of a Mr. White from Michigan. White invested $1.5 million of his own money to start a forest industry complex that included a 200-ton-per-day pulp mill, a sawmill capable of producing 100,000 board feet a day and a six-machine shingle mill.

A thriving community grew up around the

Beaver Cove was named after the paddle-wheel steamer Beaver, launched in 1835, the first steamer on the North Pacific coast. It was wrecked on Prospect Point in Vancouver in 1888. This photograph was taken in Victoria, about 1870.

mills, with a cookhouse and six bunkhouses large enough to accommodate 150 men. There was also housing for the married workmen, a hotel, and deep-sea docks. A number of immigrants from Japan and China worked at the lumber and pulp mills. It was customary in those days for them to establish their own community with their own dining room, gardens and living quarters.

Locating a plant in a remote area had many disadvantages, including the high cost of services and supplies and an unstable workforce. In 1920, the Beaver Cove Lumber & Pulp Company went into bankruptcy, and the boom town known as Englewood, which had grown up on the flats across from Beaver Cove, was empty. When the plant closed, a number of people, including Roy Hinman, Paul Gauthier, George McLean and Ed Goodrow stayed on at Beaver Cove. They homesteaded, grew their own crops, and logged and fished to supplement their incomes. In 1925, the Wood & English sawmill was built at Englewood, and a number of the former BCL&PC employees were hired. The company continued operation until 1941, logging in the Nimpkish Valley and along the Tsultan and Kokish rivers. Rail cars were used to haul the timber to the mill at Englewood.

Meanwhile, in 1926, the bankrupt Beaver Cove Lumber & Pulp Mill was taken over by a new company, Canadian Forest Products Ltd., whose principal shareholder was the International Harvester Company. Captain Corney

Above: The Nimpkish logging railway, with 100 miles of main and auxiliary line, was modernized by Canfor. It uses three 1,200 HP diesel locomotives, which haul four to five trains, carrying about one million board feet of lumber to the log dump at Beaver Cove every day.

Right: The logging railway in the Nimpkish Valley is one of the last in North America. The nine major wood trestle bridges, like the one shown here, range in height up to 148 feet.

sold the "Old Farm" to Canadian Forest Products in 1929 and returned to England. After he had gone, Mr. T.A. Swanson, an employee of CFP, moved onto the property. He added to its buildings and called it home for many years. Daffodils and daisies growing in the tall grass are all that remains of the "Old Farm" today.

Beaver Cove's first school opened in the 1920s, in one of the Canfor company houses in what was called the upper townsite. It was a one-room school where all eight grades were taught. A new school was built in 1958. The same year, the British Columbia Power Commission announced it had applied for rights to develop 35,000 hp from a new hydroelectric project on the Kokish River.

Railway logging first took place in the Nimpkish Valley in 1908 when the Nimpkish Logging Company began cutting trees around Nimpkish Lake. Canfor took over the operation in 1944, and within a decade began a major modernization program that was completed by 1957. The multi-million dollar development consisted of a campsite, railway, dumps, and a new deep-sea dock. The company already had sixty-three miles of railway into the Nimpkish Valley, as well as seventeen miles of truck road into Bonanza Lake. Logs were dumped in Nimpkish Lake and towed fourteen miles before being loaded on rail cars for the final trip to Beaver Cove. The new line ran twenty-three miles between Nimpkish and Beaver Cove. It was completed at a cost of $4.5 million. The new extension was the final link connecting the main railway to the saltwater dump at Beaver Cove.

Before modernization, Canfor's Englewood operation had as many as ten of the old steam

locomotives in service. Engine 113, a 135-ton American 2-8-2 oil-fired locie, was the largest logging locomotive in the world. It was built in 1920 for passenger service on the Portland, Astoria and Pacific Line, and (as an emergency replacement) last hauled logs in 1971, making it possibly the last working logging locomotive in North America. Locie 113 has been completely restored and was the star attraction in Canfor's fiftieth anniversary celebration in 1990. No. 112, a 90-ton Baldwin 2-6-2T manufactured in 1923, Canfor's other steam locomotive still in existence, is not operating. It is on display in front of the dryland sort office at Beaver Cove.

Following completion of the Beaver Cove

The original Locomotive No. 113 has been restored to working condition and is a major attraction at Beaver Cove. Weighing in at 135 tons, the 2-8-2 oil-fired "locie" was the largest logging locomotive in the world when it was built in 1920.

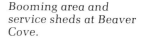

Booming area and service sheds at Beaver Cove.

Massive log booms occupy much of the shore of Beaver Cove. The mouth of the Kokish River is in the background. (George McNutt photo)

extension, three General Motors 1200-hp diesel locomotives were purchased. By 1968, one hundred miles of main and auxiliary track were utilized by the railway. Four to five trains hauling up to thirty-eight log cars each moved to the Beaver Cove dump daily, carrying about one million dollars' worth of timber to the water.

Today at Englewood, Canfor operates one of the last logging railways in North America. The long, narrow layout of the Nimpkish Valley makes it one of the few places where it is

more economical to transport logs by train than by truck.

In 1987, Canfor's Englewood Logging Division employed 475 people directly, plus 180 employed by logging contractors working for the division. The log harvest totalled 1.7 million cubic metres. Almost all the logs travelled at least part of the way to Beaver Cove by rail.

Canfor, like many big logging operations, invests a lot of money in our forest and takes a lot out. A drive through the Nimpkish Valley makes me wonder why all the mountains and

A floating crane is used to load barges with logs at Beaver Cove.

the valley floor are bare of trees, and what has happened to the animals and the birds that used to inhabit those forests. Even Beaver Cove has little left of its former wilderness. Now as you drive along the once picturesque waterfront you will see miles of railway trestles, logs in storage and log booms. Admittedly, the housing built on pilings along the water's edge and the boathouse surrounded by log booms has a certain charm. But I wondered about the birds and beavers and other wild creatures that had lived there. Today Beaver Cove looks more like the railway terminals in downtown Chicago.

Beaver Cove is not a great place to visit if you are looking for a quiet place to anchor, but it is a place to go if you want to see what is possibly the last railway logging camp in operation, as well as a couple of the old steam locies left over from another day.

The former logging settlement at Englewood, on the northwest arm of Beaver Cove, is in ruins, but there is a marina, launching ramp, sawmill, store and post office at Beaver Cove.

22. Alert Bay

Since the turn of the century, the small village of Alert Bay has played a key role in the settlement of the coast of British Columbia. It has had the hospital, the doctor, school and telecommunications service to the outside world.

Alert Bay is on the western shore of Cormorant Island, about 200 miles north of Victoria and five miles from Port McNeill. Broughton Strait separates it from the salmon-rich Nimpkish River on the northeast coast of Vancouver Island. Ferry service connects Alert Bay with Port McNeill and Sointula.

The geographical setting of Alert Bay has been described by long-time resident A.W. Wastell, in his inimitable style, as follows: "Geologists and scientists tell us that Cormorant Island, being a mass of water-worn rocks, gravel and earth, was pushed out from the mountains on the left-hand side of the Nimpkish River. This occurred millions of years ago.

"Scientists claim that Cormorant Island slid across Broughton Strait on a bed of clay about 100 feet thick. Luckily the Island didn't move further toward Malcolm Island, as the water is deeper there, and it might have disappeared, leaving only the steel masts of the Wireless Station on Cormorant still showing.

"By the time I arrived at Alert Bay in the year 1909, I found the Island pretty well set, and not showing any intention of moving further. In the interval . . . nature had grown some fine trees on the Island, but man, in his constant endeavour to advance, cut them all down, hauling them off to the sawmill for lumber, leaving only the big stumps for the next man to clear away."

I first saw Alert Bay when I was travelling to Rivers Inlet aboard the Union steamship *Cardena* in the late 1940s. It was a rainy wet day with a lot of fishermen on the dock in their oilskins; they were mostly native Indians. The *Cardena* tied alongside the BC Packers wharf to load and unload freight and passengers. The cannery was in full operation, producing the rancid odor of fish as huge white clouds of steam billowed out of its smokestacks. I was leaning over the railing watching the people on the dock and trying to see some of the town. Someone beside me was saying, "That's the Indian Reserve over there, that's the hospital, and I think that's the boys' school." I squinted, trying to see what they were talking about, but the mist was so heavy I

Street scene in Alert Bay.

could hardly see across the bay, much less make out the buildings.

Alert Bay has always been special to me, mostly because of a young Indian lad named Paul whom I met on the *Cardena*. Paul, who was about my age, was from Alert Bay. He was on his way to work in the cannery at Butedale. We played cards as he told me what it was like living on an Indian reserve. We became good friends and corresponded for a number of years.

Some years later, I was back in Alert Bay sitting on the fish dock, fascinated by an old Indian man engraving silver bracelets. His face was crinkled with age and his clothes were ragged, but his fingers worked magic as he engraved the intricate design. He smiled with eyes like dark coals. "If you have a silver dollar or two fifty-cent pieces I'll make you a bracelet like this," he said. But even if his

A cormorant-shaped grave marker surmounts a native grave at Alert Bay.

work had been a gift I didn't have the money then to spend on a bracelet.

For centuries, Cormorant Island has been home to the Kwakiutl Indians. In 1792, when Commander Dionisio Galiano, aboard the schooner *Sutil*, was approaching the island, he recorded in the ship's log: "We see a great village in the form of an amphitheatre on a hill, it is surrounded by meadows, and close to a rivulet. There are streets and the houses are painted in various hues and ornamented with good designs."

The first European settlers began moving to Cormorant Island in the 1870s. Among the early entrepreneurs on the coast at that time were two men called Huson and Spencer.

A killer whale mortuary figure marks a native grave at Alert Bay. As more and more native people converted to Christianity, burial replaced the traditional disposal of remains in "grave trees."

Though Ottawa declared potlatches illegal, this postcard from Alert Bay in the early 1900s shows piles of gifts at a very public celebration. In the "Christmas Tree" potlatch of 1921, Chief Dan Cranmer gave away 300 oak trunks, 1,000 basins, 400 Hudson's Bay blankets, 24 canoes, 4 gas boats, 1,000 sacks of flour and sugar, and huge quantities of other gifts, including guitars, violins, pool tables, dresses and shawls.

With an eye on the huge sockeye run coming into the Nimpkish River, they leased the island from the government, brought in some lumber and built a salmon saltery in Alert Bay.

Their operation wasn't too successful at first. The only available labourers were native Indians from villages around the mouth of the Nimpkish River, and the natives were often unable to go to work because they were attending celebrations in one or other of the villages. In the meantime, the saltery was short of labour until they returned. In the minds of Huson and Spencer, the solution was to get the Indians to move to Cormorant Island and settle. And one way to attract them would be to have a mission there providing medical and educational services. In 1878, the two partners prevailed on Rev. Alfred James Hall to move his

Anglican mission from Fort Rupert to Alert Bay.

Spencer and Huson also felt that instruction in the principles of Christianity would improve the work ethic of their native employees. Rev. Hall turned his home into a residential school where he and Mrs. Hall taught the native children arithmetic, music, English and the Gospel. Later Mrs. Hall carried on her work in a school built especially for girls. A boys' school had been built when the Industrial Aid Society, affiliated with the Church Missionary Society, supplied money to build a sawmill in 1887. The mill served a dual purpose in teaching the Indian boys a trade, and using the lumber they produced for houses and the new school. The Halls worked with the Indians at Alert Bay for thirty-two years, learning their language and making many friends.

Mr. and Mrs. Stephen Cook, a mixed-blood couple, became the missionaries when the Halls retired. Mrs. Cook lived to be eighty-one, and left seventy-four children, grandchildren and great-grandchildren. Many of them are active in the community today.

About 1890, the headquarters of the Indian Affairs agency for the district was moved from Fort Rupert to Alert Bay. With the preponderance of native people already living in Alert Bay, the Indian agent played a very important role in the community. The first agent, R.H. Pidcock, is credited with assisting the missionaries to build St. Michael's Residential School. He succeeded in having the government set aside 450 acres for the school, which opened in 1894 with thirty boys, under the principalship of A.W. Corker. It replaced the small school at the home of Rev. Hall.

The emphasis on industrial skills at the school was logical. The original saltery started by Huson and Spencer had been converted into a cannery in 1884, under the name of Spencer and Earle. A cannery, with its steam cooking and automatic canning line, required substantially more skills from its work force than a saltery.

Pidcock's successor as agent, William Halliday of Kingcome Inlet, seconded the activity of the Columbia Coast Mission in founding St. George's Hospital in 1909. Halliday had first gone to Alert Bay to assist Corker at the boys' residential school in 1897. He became Indian Agent in 1906.

Making Alert Bay the Indian Affairs headquarters for the district had an important influence on the development of the village. It ensured that it would become the centre for important health and educational institutions, and would continue to have a large native population, as well as a growing white population, made up of the original settlers, plus administrative, health and educational professionals serving Indian Affairs.

Some early non-native settlers were A.W. Wastell, Jim King, Dick and Chris Pattison, J.H. Skinner and Andy Gibbons. All were instrumental in turning Alert Bay into a thriving community.

Jim King was the community's first immigrant of Chinese extraction. In 1882, as a boy of eight or nine, he came to BC on an immigrant ship. Conditions on board were so bad that only half of the 142 passengers who left China survived. Jim got work in a Vancouver hotel as kitchen help and cleaner. Twenty years later, he went north to seek his fortune as a "boom man" and then as a cook in the lumber camps, which brought him enough money to return to China and marry. Back in Alert Bay, he worked in a sawmill to get money to bring his wife and child from China. Then William Halliday got him a piece of foreshore, where he started a grocery business, soon to become the best-known store in Alert Bay. Jim King sold his store in the mid-1930s to another newcomer, Dong Chong, and retired to end his days peacefully in Alert Bay. When Dong Chong moved into a smart new supermarket building in 1955, he had the satisfaction of having it designed by his son, a graduate architect from the University of British Columbia. The business is now run by his second son, Bill, a UBC commerce graduate.

In the early days, many newcomers arrived in Alert Bay by small open boat. Others came by the Union steamship vessels that served Alert Bay from the early 1890s. These vessels, with their tall red stacks, were a part of the romance surrounding the early days on the coast.

After the turn of the century many changes took place. By 1910, there was a public school, a post office, a hospital, a saloon and a hotel. The Spencer and Earle fish cannery was taken over by Henry Doyle of Vancouver and amalgamated into the new BC Packers Association. The government granted the cannery exclusive right to all the fish taken in the Nimpkish River. As well, the Industrial Aid Society sawmill had gone private, changed hands and been renamed the Alert Bay Sawmill.

The most important development was the construction of St. George's Hospital. Outside of the hospital ship *Columbia*, which had started operation in 1905, St. George's was the only medical centre on that part of the coast. The story of the hospital is interconnected with the development of the "mission ships" of the Columbia Coast Mission.

The Columbia Coast Mission, founded by the Rev. John Antle, a Church of England clergyman, played an important role along the coast during the first half of this century. In 1904, Rev. Antle conducted a survey along the Inside Passage as far north as Alert Bay to study the medical, social and religious needs

A totem pole in Alert Bay.

of the loggers and settlers. He went back to Vancouver and the following year commissioned the sixty-five-foot *Columbia* from the Wallace shipyards in False Creek. Her cabins included a small hospital and a chapel. The newly formed Missionary Society of the Church of England in Canada donated $2,000 toward her completion.

The *Columbia* serviced more than eighty logging camps. She was the ambulance of her era, and because of her, much suffering was spared and lives saved. But by 1909, the success of the *Columbia* also indicated that her unaided efforts were not sufficient to serve the medical and social needs of the growing frontier.

That same year, there was a meeting in Alert Bay at the home of Indian agent William Halliday to discuss the need for a hospital to serve the area. It was decided to ask the Rev. Antle to build a hospital in the village. BC Packers offered a one-acre site and $300 to start the project. It was typical of John Antle that he got things under way at once. His activity spurred grants from the provincial government and the Indian Affairs Department to complete the building. Furnishings were provided largely by donations from the women's auxiliaries of the Church of England across Canada.

St. George's Hospital was opened formally on June 15, 1909. M.D. Baker was the first

Above: Aerial view of Alert Bay in the 1970s, with the old native residential school in the left foreground, and ferry dock, hospital and airstrip in the background. (George McNutt photo)

Right: One of the many totem poles marking family plots in the native cemetery at Alert Bay.

doctor; Caroline D. Monk and Mary Motherwell were the first nurses. The next year, a larger *Columbia* was built to expand its service as a sea-going ambulance for the district, again thanks to the perseverance of John Antle.

Only a year after this, the federal government established a telephone-telegraph line from Campbell River to northern Vancouver Island communities, including Alert Bay. Finally, the community was in touch with "civilization."

The feel of life at Alert Bay had been quite different even a couple of years before. A.W. Wastell noted: "When I arrived in Alert Bay in 1909 it had no resemblance to what it is today [1940], except the curve of the shoreline. There was merely a path along the beach, probably a foot or two wide, from the sawmill to John Robillard's log house at the eastern end. We had no telephones, telegraph or other means of communication, except the weekly boat from what was known as the outside.

"The residences of the place were strewn along the water's edge for some mile and a half. Our road lighting consisted of a lantern in hand to guide you. Seen from the water side, these lanterns looked much like fireflies...

"On the westerly end of this long path stood the Indian Industrial School. This school was

The Alert Bay marina and docks. In the background is the old native residential school, now used as Band Council offices and educational space for North Island College.

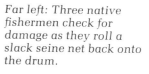

Far left: Three native fishermen check for damage as they roll a slack seine net back onto the drum.

Left: A halibut boat at dockside.

In 1915, Alert Bay consisted of a straggle of native and settlers' houses bordering a pathway along the shoreline of Cormorant Island. (CRM 10743)

The home of R.H. Pidcock, the first Indian agent resident at Alert Bay, about 1890. He retired to Quathiaski Cove in 1906. (CRM 3852)

in charge of Mr. Corker as principal, and with him were Mrs. Corker, Miss Warrener and Emily (afterwards Mrs. Cook). Between the school and the sawmill was a piece of land set aside for the use of young (native) married people who wished to live in individual houses instead of the community houses of their fathers.

"In the manager's house on the cannery property lived Mr. R. Chambers with his wife and six children. Beyond them was the house of the Provincial Constable, at that time Mr. Walter Woolacott. Next was the little public school house and then the new hospital with a staff of a doctor and a matron, one nurse, and a Chinese cook. Next to the hospital were the

residences of Dave Huson, Spence Huson and Silas Olney. Beyond that one entered a path through the woods to George Hawking's house and Jack Robillard's log cabin. Jack was boss of the fishing crew for the cannery. The foregoing were all the white residents at the time... The village was without any facilities, such as electric light or water system. Everyone had wells, mostly dry in the summer time. The outhouse was in the woods, you bathed in a tub alongside the kitchen stove, or in the ocean."

Neither the Union steamships nor the Columbia Coast Mission boats service the coast any longer. Both began to be replaced by aircraft in the late 1940s. The use of aircraft made a big change in the everyday lives of people in isolated areas. When there was a logging accident or a boating mishap, a doctor could be on the scene within minutes instead of hours or days. Dr. H.J. Pickup, known as the flying doctor, began working in the area around Alert Bay in 1949. A flying ministry began in 1960 when the United Church of Canada purchased a Cessna 170 seaplane. The plane, named the *George Pringle* in memory of one of the early marine missionaries, was first operated by Rev. Wayne Mackenzie and Rev. R. Burrows.

The great Indian village that Galiano saw in 1792 exists no longer, but the people of the Kwakiutl Nation and their hereditary Chief Billy Scow still play a major role in the development of their community. Their artists and carvers have won world acclaim and their magnificent totem poles still stand tall above the village.

Today's Alert Bay is a lively town of about 700 people, built along the waterfront with stores, hotels, restaurants, laundromats, movie theatres, a modern marina, fuel docks and all the amenities of a modern community. The U'Mista Cultural Centre houses regalia confiscated by Indian agents in the 1920s, and recently returned to the local native community by the federal government.

23. Sointula

Sointula is a fishing village on Malcolm Island, with windswept beaches and houses strung out along the water's edge. When the sun is low in the west, the crescent-shaped bay is full of light. Even the old boat sheds come to life, grey and tarnished from the weather; you know they have been there a long time.

Malcolm Island, about 185 miles north of Vancouver, lies off the northeast coast of Vancouver Island. Broughton Strait, and a twenty-minute ferry ride, separates it from Port McNeill and the first-class North Island Highway.

It is a spiritual kind of place, and in the past it has attracted people with idealistic goals. The first Europeans to settle there were a group under the guidance of a preacher named Spencer, who tried to establish a Christian community on the island in the 1890s. Isolation, conflict and poor financing caused the venture to fail.

About ten years later, another group of people dreaming of freedom and a better life moved to Sointula, under the leadership of the well-known Finnish writer and idealist Matti Kurikka. Kurikka's dream was to build a utopia for all Finns who had left Finland to escape the oppression of the Russian Tsar's rule. "In this colony a high, cultural life of freedom would be built," he wrote, "away from priests who have defiled the high morals of Christianity, away from churches that destroy peace, away from all evils of the outside!"

Kurikka had left Finland for Australia, where he had hoped to establish his colony. When a group of Finnish settlers in Nanaimo heard what he was planning, they wrote and asked him to come to British Columbia and lead them in search of freedom and a better life. After all, life in the coal mines in Nanaimo was not much better than being under the Tsar's rule. Kurikka agreed to come.

The first job was to find a suitable site for the community. The BC government gave Kurikka and his followers several choices. After poring over charts and survey maps, they made a unanimous decision to settle on Malcolm Island. The offer of such property

Left: Aerial view of Sointula shows how the community sweeps around the curving edge of Rough Bay on Malcolm Island. (George McNutt photo)

seemed too good be true. Here was 28,000 acres of rich farmland surrounded by an ocean teeming with fish and a virgin forest of cedar, spruce and hemlock. The cedar was especially fine and for centuries had provided the Nimpkish Indians with timber for their canoes, longhouses and totem poles.

It took several months to complete the negotiations for Malcolm Island. Finally, on November 27, 1901, the Kalevan Kansa Colonization Company Ltd., under the presidency of Matti Kurikka, signed an agreement to become the sole owners of Malcolm Island after seven years, provided that the 350 settlers built

The architecture of many of the wooden houses of Sointula reflects the Finnish origins of the original settlers.

Boat sheds along the beach at Sointula were once the fisherman's only protection for his boat.

*Kalevan Kansa
Colonization Company
Sointula, 1904.*

*A gravestone for the
eleven people who died
in the January 29, 1903
fire, at the Sointula
cemetery.*

homes on their eighty-acre sections and made improvements worth at least $2.50 per acre. As well, they all had to become British subjects.

Membership shares in the Kalevan Kansa Company cost $200. With the idealism expected of such a group, members had the option of substituting labour for capital if they were short of money. This ensured from the beginning that the company would be chronically short of funds.

While land negotiations were taking place, *Aika*, the Finnish newspaper that Kurikka had started in Nanaimo, kept the colonists informed. It also helped promote his utopian ideals among other Finlanders. Soon countrymen from around the world were applying for membership in the community. A.B. Makela, a writing associate of Kurikka from Finland, joined the community at this time. Makela was sworn in as secretary of the board of directors.

The first members of the colony arrived at Rough Bay, Malcolm Island, on December 14, 1901. Travelling aboard Johan Mikkelson's sailboat, they had taken over a week to get there; rain, sleet and heavy weather had slowed their progress. Others aboard included Otto Ross, Kalle Hendrickson, and Malakias Kytomaa. Theodore Tanner was in charge of the group. On shore they found shelter in an old shack built by the original religious settlers.

Heikki Kilpelainen and Viktor Saarikoski were the next to arrive on the island. Both talented woodworkers, they were sent to build a log cabin big enough to house several families. They were followed by another group that included Mr. and Mrs. Wilander, newlyweds from New York City. Anna Wilander was the first woman to come to the island. She cooked while the fourteen men built houses and cleared land.

In the spring of 1902, a steady influx of people began to arrive at Malcolm Island. To commemorate the beginning of the community, a midsummer celebration was held. Preparations for the event included building the Cedar Hall for assemblies and communal dining, and chartering the steamer *Capilano* to bring people from other parts of the coast. Many of the people who attended the celebration stayed behind to join the community.

As the summer progressed the townsite was planned, and a location for the sawmill was decided on. Sointula, meaning "harmony," was chosen as the name of the community by majority vote. Other projects got under way as well. Logging was started in Mitchell Bay, and a salmon drag-seine was purchased. That first summer went very well. It was not until the cold dampness of winter set in that the problems began. There was not enough milk for the children, nor housing for the people, nor money to start new projects.

Housing was the biggest problem. There was only one log cabin for the original work crew and the "Cedar Hall," intended as a communal dining hall. All of the new arrivals were living in tents. A new three-storey building was started in November, with a meeting room on the top floor and individual rooms for families on the two lower floors. The building was made of unseasoned wood from the island's trees cut at a new sawmill, and heated with metal pipes from a big brick stove.

In spite of the improvement in living conditions, the people were still dissatisfied with Kurikka's administration. Long, argumentative meetings were held, but there seemed to be no solution. During one such meeting on January 29, 1903, the hall caught fire. People were trapped on the second floor and two women, one man and eight children were burned to death. Arson was suspected—some claimed that Kurikka wanted to destroy the colony's ledgers—though the general view is that the fire was an accident, caused by the metal heating pipes passing through wooden walls.

Further problems arose when Kurikka and Makela clashed over a moral issue. Kurikka believed in free love, at least in theory, while most of the colonists had more conventional ideas. The disagreement was not resolved and Kurikka resigned. He left Sointula forever, taking half the community with him.

Those left behind felt deserted. Depleted in population and burdened with enormous debts, they faced a bleak future. The colonists tried to recover their losses by cutting and sawing 150,000 board feet of lumber, but on arrival in Vancouver, the lumber was misappropriated by one of the colonists who was commissioned to sell it. The creditors, hearing of this, seized the lumber, and the Kalevan Kansa Colonization Company went into receivership. All the colony's property—mainly

Left: Matti Kurikka, Finland, 1899.

Below left: Robert Turner and granddaughter Karen.

Below: Karen Turner, born at Mitchell Bay, Malcolm Island, in 1941, holds a lamb from her grandfather's farm. Robert Turner, an Australian, owned most of Mitchell Bay early in the century. His family maintains the fish-packing business he started.

Boat sheds and a boat on ways flank the government dock at Sointula. The Co-op hardware store can be seen in the background.

The foreshore at Sointula, with boat shed and spindly old jetty stretching out into the water.

In the early years, this was done from small flat-bottomed skiffs with nets belonging to the company. Motor boats twenty to thirty feet in length began to appear in the 1920s, and individual fishermen became able to own their own boats and gear. Lauri Jarvis, one of the original colonists, invented a mechanical drum for setting and hauling nets, which had been a strenuous manual task, especially in rough weather. His idea was adopted by gillnetters up and down the coast. In recent years, it has been estimated that seventy gillnetters and two dozen larger purse-seiners and trollers sail out of Sointula.

In contrast, logging operations are now carried out only on a small scale, and farming has been almost totally abandoned on the island, except for a few small producers who supply the local market.

In spite of the collapse of the colony, the people of Sointula remained committed to progressive, pro-labour ideals. The centre of the community has been the Finnish Organization Hall, where all cultural and recreational activities are held, though the activity of the organization itself has waned in recent years as the younger generation has become more assimilated into mainstream Canadian culture.

The co-operative movement has remained strong here. The first store, still the major store in town, was the Co-op, founded in 1909. It has over 300 shareholders, and is a mini-department store with several departments on two floors and a staff of eleven. The Co-op and Credit Union are both managed by Philip Au. He and his family, the only Chinese Canadians in Sointula, have lived there for twenty-two years.

Sointula has a strong local of the United Fishermen and Allied Workers Union, although about half the boats are independent now. A long strike in 1989 created friction and bitterness between union and independent fishermen.

the land and forests on Malcolm Island — was sold.

Not all was lost. There was a school, roads and houses, and a spirit that held the community together. There was work in logging camps and nearby construction sites, and the fishing was good. Putting their troubles behind them, the people of Malcolm Island worked together toward a brighter future. A.B. Makela remained with the community, serving as the local justice of the peace. Except for periods editing Finnish newspapers in the US and eastern Canada, he lived in Sointula until his death in 1932.

In the years after the collapse of the colonization company, fishing, especially gillnetting, became the major occupation on Sointula.

After the collapse of the Kalevan Kansa Colonization Company, the area around the townsite continued to develop. Only a few families settled on the more remote parts of the island. One of these was the Robert Turner family, one of the few non-Finnish families to buy property when it went on sale in 1905. They acquired some 400 acres in Mitchell Bay on the northeastern side of the island. They bought a scow and started a fish-buying business. Spence Turner, who was only two years old when his parents arrived, still lives on the bay. When his father retired, he and his wife Cathy took over the business.

In the summer of 1987, I drove down to Mitchell Bay to visit with Cathy and Spence Turner. I cannot recommend the road or the drive, but the hospitality was great! They are both retired now: Spence in 1982, and Cathy

The Co-operative store has been the mercantile centre of Sointula ever since the utopian socialist days of the Kalevan Kansa Colonization Company.

that summer. "I'd go back tomorrow if the doctor would let me," she said with a twinkle in her eye. "I miss the people and being part of that job that has been our life for so many years." They still live in their cozy cottage overlooking the ocean, where they serve coffee and spin yarns about the past to the fishermen, loggers and others who drop by for a visit.

Sointula remains a thriving community to this day, with all the conveniences of a modern town. Yet its character still represents the people who settled there in 1900. It was bathed in sunlight when I saw it last. There were the boat sheds, and fishing nets hung out to dry. Watching them get closer brought memories from long ago. I remembered that once those sheds were the only protection a fisherman had for his boat against the angry winter storms. Comparing them to the new breakwater made me think of time and changes. As I watched, I saw someone winching his boat into a shed. It was good to see the boat sheds still in use.

View of Broughton Strait from the Malcolm Inn at Sointula.

24. Port Hardy

Port Hardy, now the major population centre of North Vancouver Island, has survived repeated disaster by fire, land fraud and depression, and has always risen again from the ashes of dashed hopes. It is the stepping-off point for vessels planning to cross Queen Charlotte Sound, or for those going around Cape Scott to the west coast of the island. It is the southern terminus of the ferry run from Prince Rupert and the northern terminus of the Island Highway. The city of Victoria lies some 300 miles to the south.

The first inhabitants of this rugged stretch of coast were people of the Kwakiutl nation. They were people who lived off the sea and the area surrounding Port Hardy had everything they needed. There was an abundance of fish in the ocean and numerous mussels and clams along the beaches. As well, their villages were surrounded by the giant cedar trees they used for building their houses, canoes and furnishings. From the surrounding hills they gathered roots and berries during the summer months. They were a proud people. "Kwakiutl" means "Smoke of the World." They believed that some day the smoke from their campfires would blanket the whole earth.

The first European settlement on the northeast shore of Vancouver Island was at Beaver Harbour. There the Hudson's Bay Company established a trading post called Fort Rupert, after Prince Rupert of England, a co-founder of

the company. Having been told by the natives that there was coal in the area, the HBC conceived the idea of establishing a coal port at Fort Rupert to supply the increasing number of steamships plying the Pacific. Asked their opinion, company experts Duncan Finlayson (the original investigator of the deposit) and John Dunn advised against the idea, mainly because of the remoteness of the area and the need to protect the workers from the Indians.

However, their advice was not heeded. In the spring of 1849, HBC employees and Hawaiian labourers waded ashore at Beaver Harbour to start work on the fort, and eight Scottish miners arrived in September. Captain William McNeill, master of the *Beaver*, was in charge of the construction. By June 1850, a stockade of rough-hewn logs was in place. Bastions with rifle slits stood at two of its corners. Within the defence walls stood living quarters for twenty Englishmen, thirty French Canadians, the Hawaiians, the eight miners and their families, and a few native workmen.

The garrison cleared extra land and planted potatoes and vegetables. Fish and fresh water from a nearby stream assured their sustenance. However, things did not go well. It appears that McNeill was a disagreeable man, and a number of major errors had been made. The surface coal was no use for boiler fuel, the miners couldn't find underground coal seams, and the Indians were less than friendly.

Members of the Newhitty tribe were charged in the deaths of three British seamen in the summer of 1850. (Since the seamen were deserters, the Indians may actually have thought they were doing the HBC a favour by killing them.) The company asked the chief to produce the guilty men. The chief told John Helmcken, then in charge of the fort, that he would not give up his people but would pay compensation. This was not acceptable and Richard Blanshard, governor of Vancouver Island, ordered three boatloads of British marines to storm the Indian village.

Having advance warning of the attack, the entire village fled to Bull Harbour on Nigei Island, fifteen miles farther up the coast. When the marines found the village abandoned, they set fire to the houses and followed the Indians to Bull Harbour, where they burned the new village as well. This time, the Newhitties gave the British the bodies of three of their slain men, who they named as the murderers, and

Port Hardy in 1920. At left is part of the church, and on the hilltop is the Bayview Hotel.

Lyon home and government wharf, 1916. Tex Lyon was born here in 1911.

the British accepted this gesture. However, Blanshard's strong-arm policy toward the Indians won him no points in London, and before long he resigned, to be replaced in 1851 by the Chief Factor of the HBC in Victoria, James Douglas.

Trouble at Fort Rupert continued, and by 1860 its population was reduced to eight hardy individuals. Attempts at coal mining had ceased, but the company was continuing to trade for furs with the Indians. The isolation of the settlement worked against it, however. Fort Rupert lay some 200 miles north of the nearest settlement, Nanaimo, and its only contact with the world was twice a year when the *Beaver* came to load furs and bring supplies. It was a losing operation for the HBC.

In 1873, the company sold its holdings to Robert Hunt, the former factor of the post. On May 27, 1889, the post burned to the ground, leaving only a chimney to mark the site of the North Island's first settlement.

Hunt continued to live at Fort Rupert, operating a small store servicing the prospectors, hand-loggers and trappers who came in occasionally by rowboat. The desolate ruin of the old fort was not an attractive place, and few stayed around for very long. One who did stay was Alec Lyon, a Scottish mechanic who arrived at Fort Rupert the year it burned, and met and married Sarah Hunt, Robert's daughter. After their marriage, they lived at Beaver Harbour for a few years, then decided to move a few miles up the coast to Hardy Bay, where there was an abandoned house they could take over near the government wharf. It had been used as a post office and store.

As Sarah was very pregnant, the Lyons were anxious to move into their new home. However, when they landed, Sarah stumbled and went into premature labour. After making her as comfortable as he could, Alec took a canoe and returned to Fort Rupert for help. But luck wasn't with him. Soon after he left, a

Above: The Lyon family, 1915. Parents with (left to right) Annie, Douglas, James, Robert, Margaret (in rear) and Allan (Tex).

Left: Mr. and Mrs. Alec Lyon displaying fresh-caught salmon, 1920.

Above: In season, the harbour at Port Hardy is jammed with every type of fishing boat, old and new.

Right: Jack Randall, born at Quathiaski Cove, was married for the first time at age 81, and lives aboard his boat at Port McNeill.

Far right: The government dock at Port Hardy, on the way down to the floats, crowded with pleasure and fishing craft.

storm blew in and he was unable to get back with help for Sarah for two days. When he did return, he found her lying on the floor of the cabin with her first-born lying by her side. The Lyons were Port Hardy's first residents, and Douglas Alec Lyon, their son, was its first baby.

In the fall of 1988, I was fortunate enough to meet Allen (Tex) Lyon, the youngest son of Alec and Sarah. Tex spent most of his working years as a wharfinger in Port Hardy, as well as with the Union Steamship Company. Since re-

tiring, he spends most of his time working in the garden, feeding the birds, walking on the beach and writing a column for the North Island *Gazette* called "Strait Talk." I shared a wonderful afternoon with Tex in his cozy cottage looking over Story's Beach in Beaver Harbour, not far from where his mother and father had met and fallen in love before the turn of the century. A stiff southeasterly wind was blowing up the strait that day. The gulls screeched, flying hard against the strong gusts, as a thundering ocean rolled up on the beach out front.

"You should see it when it is really blowing and the waves come right up against the window," said Tex. The day was wild and beautiful and it was easy to understand why Tex had chosen to continue to live on that part of the coast.

During the afternoon Tex told me about some of the changes that had taken place in Port Hardy since the early days. About his parents, he said: "After their traumatic arrival, they had planned to start a store. But the *Boscowitz*, the vessel bringing their entire stock, foundered and sank in Queen Charlotte Sound." Along with their stock went Alec Lyon's life savings. They still had a $2,000 legacy left to Sarah by her father. They used this money to re-order the stock, and this time it arrived safely.

Lyon's Trading Post opened only a few weeks behind schedule. At first the only customers were the Kwakiutl, who traded furs and dried fish for blankets, bullets and tinned

goods. However, there were more than a hundred prospectors working in the area, and business soon picked up. They began using the post as their headquarters for mail and supplies.

Between 1904 and 1912, it was Sarah and Alec Lyon who provided most of the increase in population. Their son James was born in 1906, followed by Robert in 1907, Margaret in 1908 and Allen (Tex) in 1911. The only other settlers at the time were the Grierson brothers and Tom Harris, who was there part time.

The permanent population of the village of Port Hardy was one family and a trading post at the beginning of 1912. By the end of the year, the statistics were quite different, thanks to the Hardy Bay Lands Company, a fraudulent company that sold nonexistent land. It was located in Vancouver near the old tram station on Hastings, where newcomers to the

Above: God's Pocket is a tiny protected bay on Hurst Island near Christie Pass, ten miles west of Port Hardy, where boaters can anchor before entering the choppy waters of Queen Charlotte Sound.

Left: Harry Kerr and Molly Milroy have carved a cozy fishing and diving resort out of the rocks protecting God's Pocket.

Street scene in Port Hardy, c. 1930.

city would notice its flashy sign advertising wonderful land at rock-bottom prices. The HBLC advertised in newspapers in the USA and England as well as in British Columbia. Its advertisements described Port Hardy as a prosperous seaport with rail yards and grain elevators. This sales pitch was illustrated by pictures of rich farmlands and attractive homes. As well, there were newspaper clippings about the great future of Port Hardy, then listed in official directories as the terminus of the Island Railway.

The owners of the HBLC were swindlers of the worst kind, who lived off the misfortunes of the poor. Their company was listed in the Vancouver City Directory only for the year 1913. By 1914, the owners had disappeared without a trace, along with their victims' savings. Most of the dupes were newcomers to the west coast, who had no idea what the country was like. Many of them had given every cent they had to the HBLC, only to discover when they arrived in Port Hardy that

they owned a few acres of bush or rock. One man found his land was in the middle of Hardy Bay! Few of them had enough money to get back to Vancouver. Some of the men tried fishing or trapping, others obtained grants of Crown land on which they tried to eke out a living. The only good thing one could say for the HBLC is that it boosted Port Hardy's population to twelve families.

Along with the increase in population came new services. In 1913, a telegraph line was strung through the woods from Campbell River to Lyon's store. As well, a number of small industries were in operation. Among them was the sawmill that supplied the town with lumber for houses and for its first school. Finding enough children for a school was always a problem, and in 1915 Tex Lyon found himself enrolled at the age of four so that the school could open. Lumber from the mill was also used to build the town's first church. The Rev. Arnold Stackhouse was the first minister. His charge was virtually the whole North Is-

Port Hardy Hotel, 1945. My sister Louise is second from right, leaning against the hitching post.

land from Cape Scott to Hardy Bay.

The 120-room Bayview Hotel opened its doors in 1918. The three-storey complex towered above the little town like a medieval castle. By 1919, Port Hardy village consisted of a church, two general stores, a mill, a hotel, a few good homes and a number of bachelor shacks. There were twenty-three families with twelve school-aged children living there.

In the early 1920s, when construction of the pulp mill at Port Alice on the west coast of the island was under way, a first-class road was built from Port Hardy to Coal Harbour.

Port Hardy got a new government wharf in 1924. The only problem was that the wharf was built on the west side of the bay, opposite the town. The business community relied on freight shipments by boat, and moved across the bay in order to survive. The next year, Alec Lyon built his store and post office alongside the new wharf, and his competitor, A.E. Smith, opened up across the street. A third store was started in 1928 by Harry Cadwallader, a descendant of the original Robert Hunt of Fort Rupert. That same year, John Nicholson opened the Hardy Bay, the first hotel on the west bank, and a year later the Seacrest opened its doors. By then, with the exception of a few "old timers," the entire village had moved to the west bank, or "new Port Hardy."

There were 142 people living in Port Hardy when the Great Depression of the 1930s came along. The people there struggled for survival like everyone else, maintaining their high morale by working on community projects. It was during that time they built the community hall with lumber from the dismantled Cholberg fish cannery in Shushartie Bay.

When World War II broke out, the government built an air base in Holberg Inlet, thirty miles west of Port Hardy. The airport was converted to civilian use in 1946, and there were daily flights in and out of town. With this improvement in communications, Port Hardy continued to grow. By 1948 the population had reached 772.

By 1966, the district of Port Hardy was incorporated, and soon after one of the old prospectors who had been roaming the coast for years discovered a massive deposit of high-grade copper in Rupert Inlet. The claim was sold to Utah Construction and Mining Company, which began operations in 1969, employing 500 men. By 1977, the population of Port Hardy was over 4,000, with three hotels, two theatres, two supermarkets, a hospital and clinic, four churches, several banks, a swimming pool and a number of restaurants.

By the end of the decade, the North Island Highway was completed, and a major port facility at Bear Cove on the east bank of Hardy Bay was in operation, making Port Hardy the southern terminal for the Vancouver Island–Prince Rupert ferry run. The terminal building

A plank logging road outside Port Hardy, at junction to Port Alice, 1945.

is located a few yards up the beach from where Alec and Sarah Lyon landed seventy-four years earlier.

Today Fort Rupert is part of the District of Port Hardy. The chimney of the old fort, built by Hawaiian servants for Scottish miners in 1849, still stands. It is now the focus of a municipal park, where May Day and other special celebrations are held.

Visitors may want to take a walk along the "Tex Lyon Trail." Commencing at the boat launch at Beaver Harbour Park, the path leads through the trees and along the beach to Dillon Point, looking over the Queen Charlotte Straits and the historic site of Fort Rupert. Tex Lyon, known as "Mr. Port Hardy," is an amateur naturalist, and there are many species of birds, wildflowers, and trees native to the North Island along the trail named for him.

Back in Port Hardy, visitors will find all the amenities of a thriving modern town. For the boater there are several marinas, good haul-out facilities, and marine repair shops. Whether you visit by land or sea, Port Hardy is a great base from which to explore the numerous points of interest along the north coast.

Eddie Carlsen with a load of logs, Port Hardy, 1941.

25. Cascade Harbour · Shushartie Bay

The story of many a coastal village is the story of the men and women who settled the site. At the turn of the century there were many such places, most now abandoned and overgrown. Such is the case with two small settlements at the north end of windswept Vancouver Island, founded by pioneers, deserted once the founders moved on.

Shushartie Bay on the northeastern shore of Vancouver Island was settled by Jepther James Skinner and H. Shuttleworth in 1906. While Shuttleworth moved on to homestead at Cape Commerel (renamed Cape Sutil), Jepther, known as J.J., married Eileen Godkin, whose family was living near Port Hardy, and the pair bought the Shushartie Bay Trading Post. Sometimes called the Shushartie Hotel, the trading post included a store and post office as well as a few sleeping rooms. The Skinners also farmed the land and brought in livestock. They enlarged the trading post by adding an extra building and installing floats so that small vessels could tie up. For the first few years, much of their trade was with the Indians from the Newhitty Reserve on Hope Island, especially when a potlatch was about to take place.

Excine, the Skinners' only child, was born in 1921 while the family lived in Shushartie.

She now lives at Qualicum Beach on Vancouver Island and has no desire to move back to Shushartie. J.J. Skinner died at his home after a lengthy illness. His ashes were scattered over the sea from the decks of the Mission boat *Columbia* in a service held off Pine Island Light. Eileen Skinner sold Shushartie Bay in the early 1940s and moved to Vancouver. In 1952, she married Captain Ed Godfrey, skipper of the *Columbia*.

Eileen sold the trading post to a remarkable man named Christian Cholberg, a self-taught genius at ship design and shipbuilding. Christian Cholberg had left home at the age of sixteen to work the big cargo ships that were plying the oceans under sail. When he first arrived on the west coast, he settled in Astoria, Oregon. There was boatbuilding and fishing in Astoria, and most people made their living from the sea. Christian felt at home there, as it reminded him of the fishing village he had left behind in Norway.

Though he no longer sailed on the windjammers, he still worked with them, crewing on the pilot tugs that hauled them up the Columbia River to unload freight in Portland. He worked with the river tugs for a couple of years before joining a San Francisco-based shipping company that was going north to

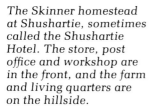

The Skinner homestead at Shushartie, sometimes called the Shushartie Hotel. The store, post office and workshop are in the front, and the farm and living quarters are on the hillside.

The Canadian Fishing Company cannery at Cascade Harbour closed shortly after the turn of the century.

Bristol Bay, Alaska to set up a fishball cannery. The outfit left in the spring of 1909 and was in Bristol Bay within six weeks. A month later, the cannery was built and ready to go into operation.

Bristol Bay was a sharp contrast to Astoria and San Francisco. Instead of lush farmlands, the ground was permafrost surrounded by stark, glacier-clad mountains, and the cold and often stormy Bering Sea. The crew used the long daylight hours in the summer months to fish and can around the clock. By the time the winter storms were brewing, they were already on their way south with a hold full of canned fishballs.

Christian spent a couple of years in the canning business before returning to Astoria to settle and marry Astrid Torp. He next turned his hand to shipbuilding, a craft that had been in his family for centuries. It was not long before the genius of Christian Cholberg began to show. The young man knew every detail of the ships on which he had sailed, and his drawings of them were so perfectly executed that other ships could be built from them. It was this reputation that landed him a job with the Foundation Company Yard in Victoria, to finish the wooden ships they were building.

Christian Cholberg moved to Victoria with his wife and two sons, Irwin and Arthur. When the job with the Foundation Company finished, he took another contract to build three large schooners for the Norwegian government, the *Gunn*, the *Vancouver* and the *Washington*. About 200 feet in length, they were designed, built and rigged under Cholberg's supervision. He then contracted to build three barquentines for a new company called Victoria Ship Owners Ltd.

Cholberg was a perfectionist, and the best of material went into these ships. Unfortunately, they were so well-built that they cost twice the

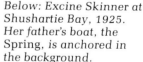

Left: Eileen Skinner cools her bread on a sunny afternoon at Shushartie Bay in the early 1920s.

Below: Excine Skinner at Shushartie Bay, 1925. Her father's boat, the Spring, is anchored in the background.

Launching
S.F. Tolmie
Dec 28th 1920

estimated amount to build. This and other factors forced Victoria Ship Owners into bankruptcy, and Cholberg's own yard went into receivership as well. The 500 men he had working for him were suddenly without jobs. Of the three ships ordered, only the *Tolmie* was finished and put in sea-time. The others were broken up and sold as firewood.

In spite of the difficult times, Christian Cholberg was not disillusioned. Taking what money he had left, he moved his family to Vancouver, where he opened the Venus Cannery at the foot of Main Street and went back into the fishball business. The operation was successful until the crash of 1929, when once again he lost everything. This time Cholberg managed to buy a scow, on which he built a two-storey house. The upper storey was living quarters, and on the lower deck he fitted an Ottessen freezing plant for preserving fish in brine. He first took the barge to Prince Rupert, then moved it down to Alert Bay. Cholberg froze fish during his first summer there. He then beached the barge and moved to Cascade Harbour, where he went back into the boat-building business.

There were a number of other people living at Cascade Harbour while the Cholbergs were there. Ernie Brown had a sawmill and cut lumber for Cholberg, who eventually bought the old Schibler mill at Owen Bay and brought it around to Cascade. He built a number of

Above: Launching the Tolmie in 1920.

Left: Mrs. Christian Cholberg, in Victoria at the christening of the Tolmie.

Some of the 500 men working at the Foundation Company Yard in Victoria under the direction of Christian Cholberg.

Left: BC dignitaries at the launching of the Tolmie in Victoria. Mrs. Christian Cholberg, holding flowers, is near the centre.

Overleaf: The Cholberg Ship Yard in Victoria produced three schooners just after World War One. The construction of the three barquentines led to bankruptcy for the firm; only the Tolmie was launched. The other two ships were broken up for firewood.

The Union Steamship vessel Camosun *entering Shushartie Bay, 1924.*

fishing boats in his yard at Cascade Harbour, including one of Fred Kohse's first boats, the *B.C. Troller.*

Another settler in Cascade at that time was Art Jones, an Australian, who had a boat called the *Dingo* and kept a store and fish camp, and sold Home Oil products. A part-time resident was Chris Wag, who had the seiners *Antler* and *Mollie-May.* He kept a fish pond in Cascade Harbour during the summer months and sold live bait to halibut boats.

When the war broke out in 1939, twenty-four-year-old Irwin Cholberg, who had been working with his father building boats, enlisted in the service. Christian and Astrid moved to Shushartie Bay, where the Union steamship called twice a week, so they would not be as isolated. The Cholbergs bought the Jepther Skinner property at Shushartie, which included the building known as "the hotel." It had seven rooms and provided a place to sleep for people travelling to the outer islands.

Cholberg planned to continue boatbuilding at Shushartie and in addition to a boatbuilding shed, he built a marine ways big enough to hold a sixty-ton vessel. However, his health was poor, and outside of rebuilding the fishing vessel *New Fraser,* his boatbuilding

The New Fraser was rebuilt at Shushartie Bay by Christian Cholberg in 1945.

Above: Looking over Cascade Harbour on Nigei Island. (George McNutt photo)

Left: The original lighthouse on Pine Island, Queen Charlotte Sound, in 1958, before it was destroyed by hurricane-force winds. It was rebuilt and continues to be one of the most important manned lighthouses on the coast.

Drawing of the Tolmie *under sail, by marine artist Noël Day.*

days were finished. Christian Cholberg was sixty-nine years old when he died. His son Irwin had married and moved to New Westminster after returning from his war service. Astrid died in 1942, shortly after the Cholbergs made the move to Shushartie. Their youngest son Arthur died in Victoria as a youngster. Irwin Cholberg died in the winter of 1991, after a lengthy illness.

Irwin Cholberg sold the land at Shushartie Bay to a logging outfit in the 1960s. The company moved in, clear-cut all of the timber and then moved on. Consequently the land came back to Irwin. It was recently sold to an Englishman, T.H.R. Chambers, who had already bought land at Cascade Harbour. It is his retirement haven and he loves the solitude.

The *Tolmie* died six years before her builder. She was the last of the big windjammers built in British Columbia, and there are many legends about her. According to sea lore, when a man dies while working on a ship under construction, she is doomed before her launching. The spirit of the dead man is believed to take the helm of the ship, and the place where he died will also be the resting place of the ship. Such a ship will never want to leave her home port.

The *Tolmie* finished her sailing days in 1929. After making several trips across the Pacific, she worked as a herring saltery off the west coast. Eventually she was turned into a log barge. Her battered hull bore only a slight resemblance to the beautiful sailing ship she once was. During a raging southeaster, she broke her moorings off Ogden Point and threw herself against the ragged rocks of Macaulay Point, resisting the efforts of tugs to remove her. Old-timers said it was suicide. She was judged a wreck and burned for her copper.

A few months later, a man looking for firewood noticed a plank banging up against the dock where the Cholberg Marine Ways had once stood. When he pulled the waterlogged piece of lumber onto the dock, he saw the name *Tolmie* carved deep into the wood.

Models of the *Tolmie* can be seen at the Vancouver Maritime Museum and the British Columbia Maritime Museum in Victoria. Cholberg Point at the entrance to Cascade Harbour, and a monument in Victoria erected to commemorate the building of the *Tolmie*, are permanent reminders of Christian Cholberg, a very talented man.

Epilogue

Today when I travel by boat along the coast of British Columbia I am struck by the changes that have taken place. There are no longer Union Steamship vessels or small supply ships travelling these waters. Today people travel in their own boats, by charter vessel or by float plane. There are fly-in resorts and fish farms, but many of the early settlers and their descendants have moved, and the villages they created have disappeared.

Some of these villages gave way to economic activities in the area. What was once my family's homestead on Quadra Island has been logged off by one of the "timber giants." It is now another barren section of the coast, devoid of every tree except for a few snags. The grassy meadows where our goats once grazed, and the fertile soil where fruit trees, vegetables and flowers once grew, were bulldozed under and used as a log dump. Even the shiny white offshore rock we named "Seagull Rock," where we played as children, was blasted into the sea.

But there are still reminders of the early settlements along the coast: an old cabin on the beach or a rosebush clinging to a crumbling trellis. It has been my good fortune to spend many summers visiting these forgotten bays and inlets along the B.C. coast, and to dip into the rich history of the area. As we lay at anchor one warm summer evening in one of these mystic harbours, I wrote in my diary:

"On the shore behind the anchorage is an old log cabin, barely visible through the underbrush and trees. The atmosphere is haunted with memories from long ago. The silence is broken only by the call of a kingfisher and a raven echoing in the hills. The distant mountains are a faint blue. Light green deciduous trees stand near the shore in front of the dark evergreens that once surrounded the old homestead. It is the beauty of solitude that one longs for.

"I take the dinghy and row around the perimeter of the sheltered harbour, listening to the sound of the oars dipping into the water and watching a salmon jump toward its spawning stream at the head of the bay. A couple of golden eagles perched on a branch

One of the many picturesque harbours where I have been touched by the vanishing history of the coast.

watch me as I pull the dinghy onto the beach at an old homestead on the far side of the bay. I have an eerie feeling walking through the tall grass and seeing the daisies in full bloom, all that remains of what once was someone's treasured garden. I feel that I am trespassing on the secret places of a departed generation. I return to the dinghy on the beach."

When I visit these abandoned places I am awed by the years of history that can still be felt around them. I ask myself: "Who once lived here? What were they like? Why did they choose to live here? And what became of them?"

In researching and writing this book I have tried to answer some of these questions, for myself and for anyone who explores the British Columbia coast—still one of the world's most mystical and beautiful places.

Sources

I.   Books and Monographs

Andersen, Aili. *The History of Sointula*. N.p., n.d.

Andersen, Doris. *Evergreen Islands*. Sydney, BC: Gray's Publishing, 1979.

Chappell, John. *Cruising Beyond Desolation Sound*. Vancouver: Naikoon Marine, 1979.

Duncan, Frances, and Rene Harding. *Sayward (for Kelsey Bay)*. Cloverdale, BC: D.W. Friesen and Sons, 1979.

Forester, Joseph E. and Anne D. *Fishing: BC's Commercial Fishing Industry*. Saanichton: Hancock House, 1975.

Gold, Wilmer. *Logging As It Was*. Victoria: Morriss Publishing, 1985.

Gould, Ed. *BC's Logging History*. Saanichton: Hancock House, 1975.

Healey, Elizabeth. *A History of Alert Bay and District*. N.p., n.d.

Hill, Beth. *Upcoast Summers*. Ganges: Horsdal & Schubart, 1985.

Hilson, Steve. *Exploring Puget Sound and British Columbia*. Auburn, WA: Publishing Enterprises, 1981.

Kennedy, Liv, and Lorraine Harris. *Vancouver Once Upon a Time*. Vancouver: CJOR Radio, 1974.

Landale, Zoe. *Harvest of Salmon*. Saanichton: Hancock House, 1977.

Lewis, David. *Yesterday's Promises: A History of the District of Port Hardy*. Victoria, n.d.

Richter, Phil. *Guide to Blind Channel and Surroundings*. Blind Channel, BC: Blind Channel Trading Co., 1988.

Walbran, Capt. John T. *British Columbia Place Names, 1592–1906*. Vancouver: J.J. Douglas, 1971.

White, Howard, and Jim Spilsbury. *Spilsbury's Coast*. Madeira Park, BC: Harbour Publishing, 1987.

Wolferstan, Bill. *Pacific Yachting's Cruising Guide to British Columbia, vol. II: Desolation Sound*. Vancouver: Maclean-Hunter, Special Interest Publications, 1980.

II.   Periodicals

Greene, Rev. Alan. "It's quite a business getting to Hospital," *The Log*, vol. II, no. 8, p. 2.

Dickie, Francis. "Forest Fire Book Choice," *The Daily Colonist* (Victoria), July 30, 1967, p. 4.

Clarke, Cecil. "Read Island Mystery," *The Daily Colonist* (Victoria), Feb. 19, 1978, p. 4.

Index